The Only
Chord Book
You Will Ever Need!
Piano • Keyboard

Editors: Steve Gorenberg & John McCarthy
Supervising Editor: Cathy McCarthy
Music Transcribing & Engraving: Jimmy Rutkowski
Production Manager: John McCarthy
Photography: Nick Finelli

AUDIO Engineering & Recording
Jimmy Rutkowski, Sal Grillo,
Mark Manczuk & John McCarthy

Cover Art Direction & Design:
Paul Enea, Tovero & Marks

HL00127047
ISBN: 9784-4803-8772-0

table of contents

how to use this book

This chord reference book contains a collection of the most popular chords for the keyboard in every key. The included CDs contain tracks that correspond to each chord. On the CDs, you will hear each chord played, followed by the notes of the chord played separately. The track numbers on the CDs correspond directly to the numbers above each chord in this book, giving you a convenient reference. Disc 1 contains the chords in the keys of C, Db, D, Eb, E and F. Disc 2 contains the chords in the keys of F#, G, Ab, A, Bb and B.

Each chord is represented using music notation, a photo and an illustration. The photo shows the correct hand position for each chord. In each illustration, the keys played are colored in gray and the note names are indicated above or below each key. The keys are numbered to indicate the suggested fingerings for each chord (1 = thumb, 2 = index, 3 = middle, 4 = ring, 5 = pinky).

This Rock House product offers FREE membership to our interactive lesson support site. Register at www.rockhousemethod.com using the member number located on the inside back cover of this book. Once registered, you can use this fully interactive site to access and download additional content, including backing tracks to jam along with and an advanced keyboard chord section containing an additional 72 chords. You can also link with instructors, explore other rock house products and connect with a community of musicians around the world who are learning to play using The Rock House Method.

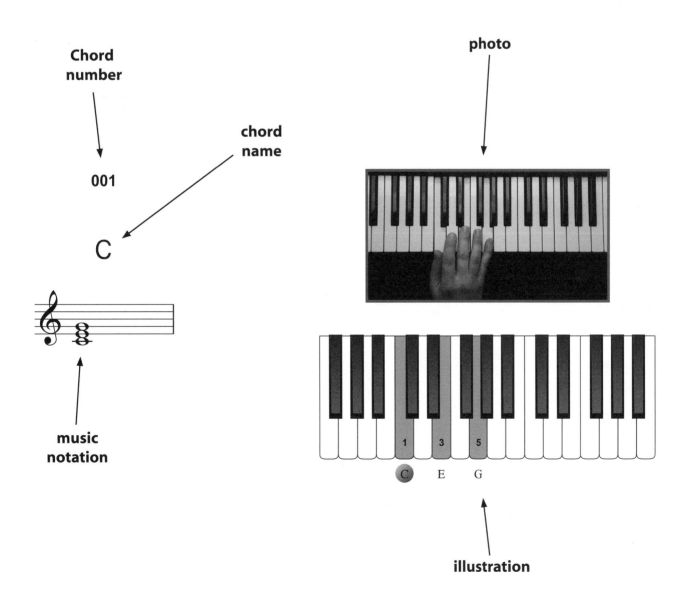

Chord number

chord name

photo

001

C

music notation

illustration

chords used in this book

major

C

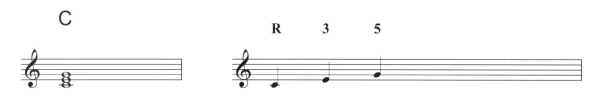

augmented

C+

suspended fourth

C^{SUS4}

major sixth

C⁶

dominant seventh

C⁷

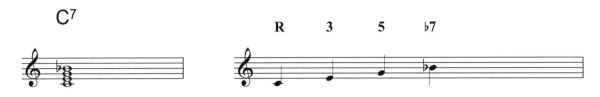

diminished seventh

C^{o7}

major seventh

Cmaj⁷

minor

Cm

minor sixth

Cm⁶

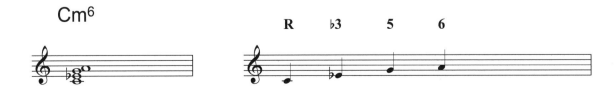

minor seventh

Cm⁷

minor seventh flat-five

Cm⁷♭⁵

dominant seventh flat-nine

C⁷♭⁹

dominant seventh sharp-nine

C⁷♯⁹

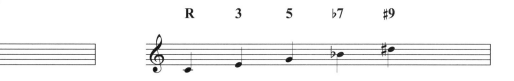

dominant ninth

C⁹

dominant ninth suspended four

dominant ninth flat-five

dominant ninth sharp-eleven

dominant thirteenth

dominant thirteenth flat-five

dominant thirteenth flat-nine

C¹³♭9

dominant thirteenth sharp-nine

C¹³♯9

dominant thirteenth flat-five flat-nine

C¹³♭5♭9

dominant thirteenth flat-five sharp-nine

C¹³♭5♯9

dominant thirteenth sharp-five flat-nine

C¹³♯5♭9

dominant thirteenth sharp-five sharp-nine

C¹³#5#9

major six/nine

C⁶⁄₉

major ninth

Cmaj⁹

major ninth sharp-eleven

Cmaj⁹#11

major thirteenth

Cmaj¹³

major thirteenth flat-five

Cmaj^{13♭5}

major thirteenth sharp-five

Cmaj^{13♯5}

major thirteenth flat-nine

Cmaj^{13♭9}

major thirteenth sharp-nine

Cmaj^{13♯9}

minor seventh flat-nine

Cm^{7♭9}

minor ninth

Cm⁹

minor eleventh

Cm¹¹

The Major Scale Chord Formula

The major scale chord chart on the following page can be used to create songs and chord progressions in any major key. This chart gives you a shortcut to the knowledge and music theory used to write music in any key. Use the tips below to help you in the process.

1) Every chord in the scale can be simplified from its full seventh form to smaller versions:

> **major 7 → major → root + five**
> **minor 7 → minor → root + five**
> **dominant 7 → major → root + five**
> **minor 7 flat five → diminished → root + flat five**

2) The three principal chords in any key are the I - IV - V chords. These chords form the most solid chord structure within progressions.

3) Every major key has a relative minor key that begins on the sixth degree of the major key. By using the process below, you can create chord scales for every minor key as well.

	1	2	3	4	5	**6**	7
Key of C major:	Cmaj7	Dm7	Em7	Fmaj7	G7	**Am7**	Bm7♭5

	1	2	3	4	5	6	7
Key of A minor:	**Am7**	Bm7♭5	Cmaj7	Dm7	Em7	Fmaj7	G7

	I	ii	iii	IV	V	vi	vii°
C	Cmaj7	Dm7	Em7	Fmaj7	G7	Am7	Bm7♭5
G	Gmaj7	Am7	Bm7	Cmaj7	D7	Em7	F♯m7♭5
D	Dmaj7	Em7	F♯m7	Gmaj7	A7	Bm7	C♯m7♭5
A	Amaj7	Bm7	C♯m7	Dmaj7	E7	F♯m7	G♯m7♭5
E	Emaj7	F♯m7	G♯m7	Amaj7	B7	C♯m7	D♯m7♭5
B	Bmaj7	C♯m7	D♯m7	Emaj7	F♯7	G♯m7	A♯m7♭5
F♯	F♯maj7	G♯m7	A♯m7	Bmaj7	C♯7	D♯m7	E♯m7♭5
D♭	D♭maj7	E♭m7	Fm7	G♭maj7	A♭7	B♭m7	Cm7♭5
A♭	A♭maj7	B♭m7	Cm7	D♭maj7	E♭7	Fm7	Gm7♭5
E♭	E♭maj7	Fm7	Gm7	A♭maj7	B♭7	Cm7	Dm7♭5
B♭	B♭maj7	Cm7	Dm7	E♭maj7	F7	Gm7	Am7♭5
F	Fmaj7	Gm7	Am7	B♭maj7	C7	Dm7	Em7♭5

001

C

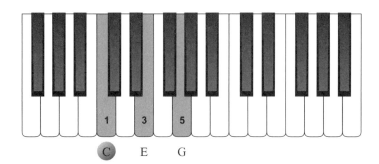

002

C+

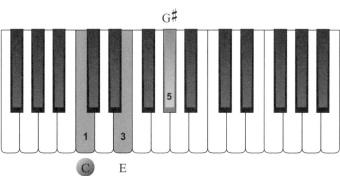

003

Csus4

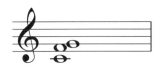

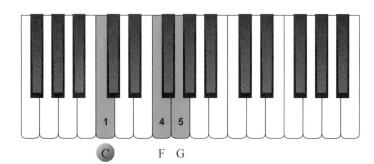

004

C^6

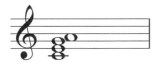

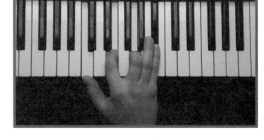

C   E   G   A

005

C^7

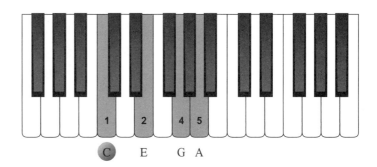

B♭

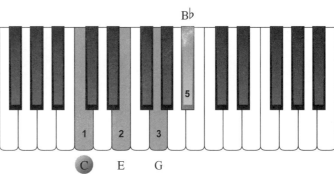

C   E   G

006

C^{O7}

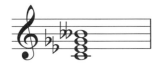

E♭   G♭

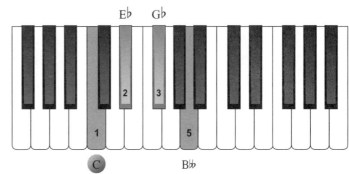

C   B♭♭

007

Cmaj⁷

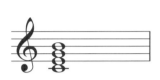

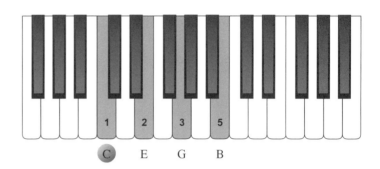

008

Cm

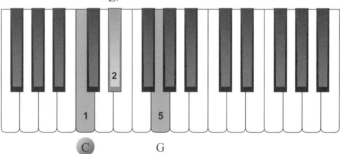

009

Cm⁶

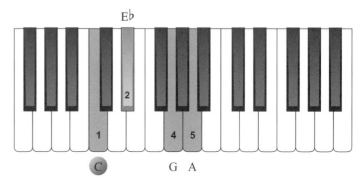

010

Cm⁷

011

Cm⁷♭⁵

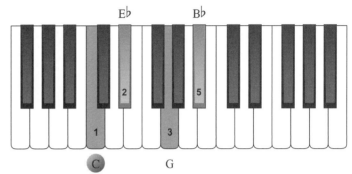

012

C⁷♭⁹

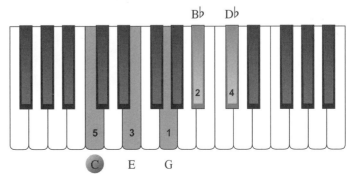

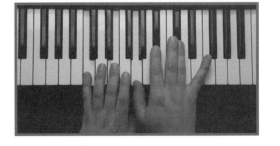

013

C⁷♯⁹

014

C⁹

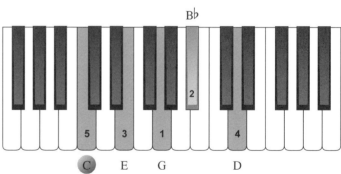

015

C⁹SUS4

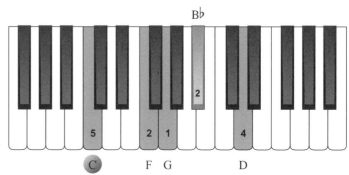

016

$C^{9\flat5}$

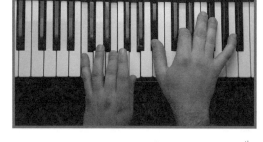

017

$C^{9\sharp11}$

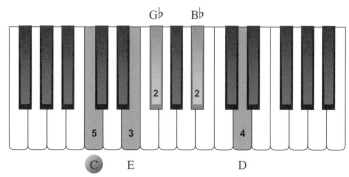

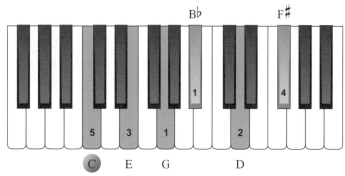

018

C^{13}

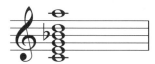

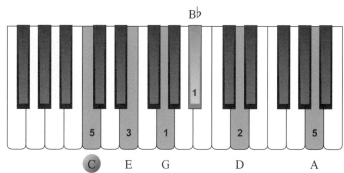

019

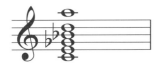

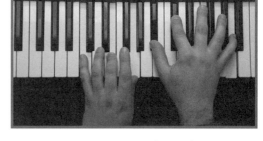

020

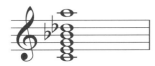

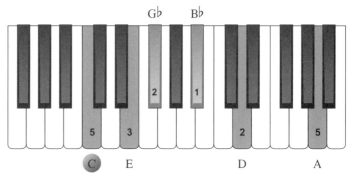

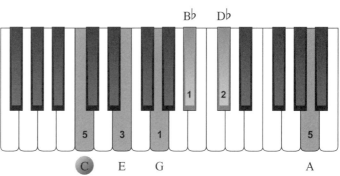

021

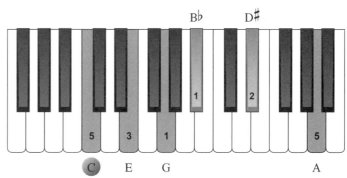

022

$C^{13\flat5\flat9}$

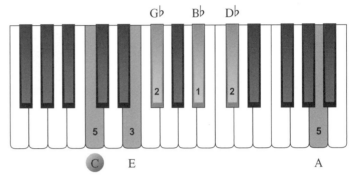

023

$C^{13\flat5\sharp9}$

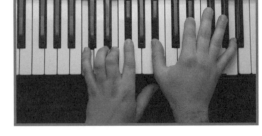

024

$C^{13\sharp5\flat9}$

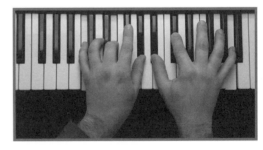

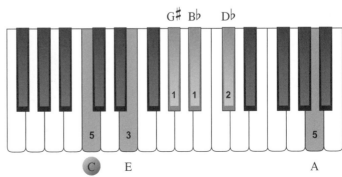

025

C¹³#5#9

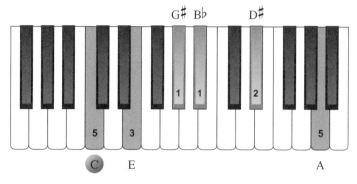

026

C⁶⁄₉

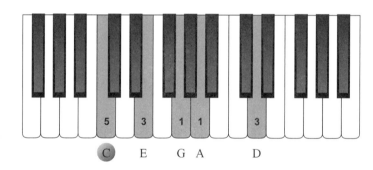

027

Cmaj⁹

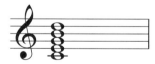

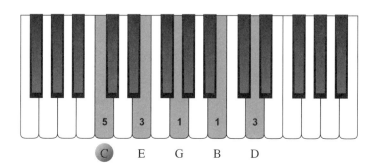

028

Cmaj^{9#11}

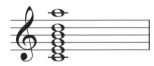

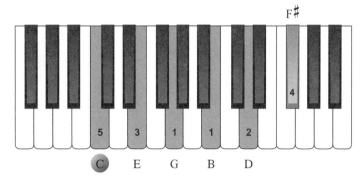

029

Cmaj¹³

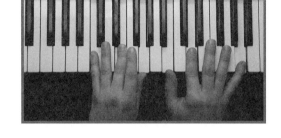

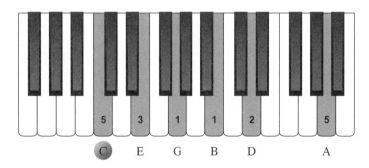

030

Cmaj^{13♭5}

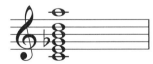

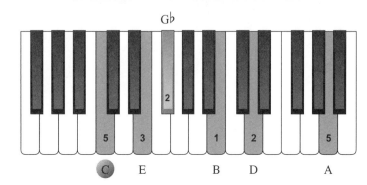

031

Cmaj^{13♯5}

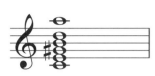

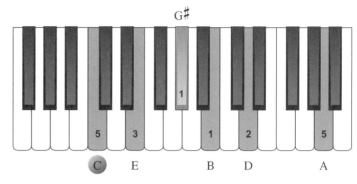

032

Cmaj^{13♭9}

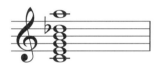

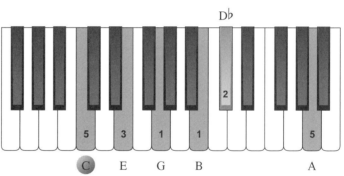

033

Cmaj^{13♯9}

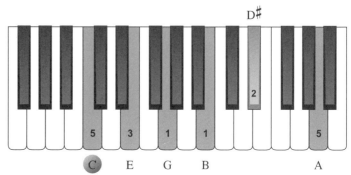

034

Cm$^{7\flat9}$

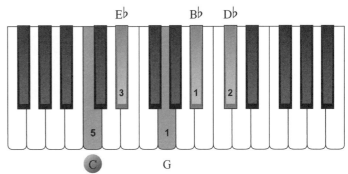

035

Cm^{9}

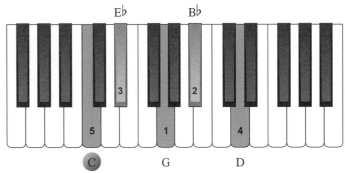

036

Cm^{11}

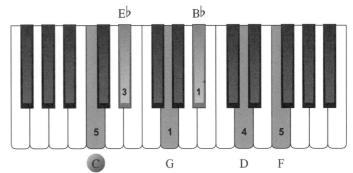

037

D♭

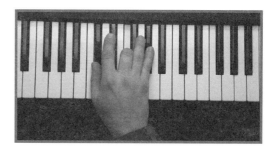

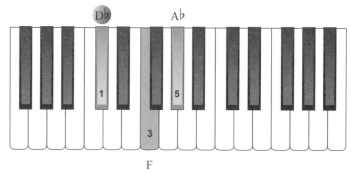

038

D♭+

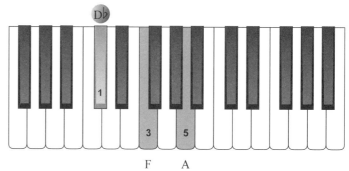

039

D♭sus4

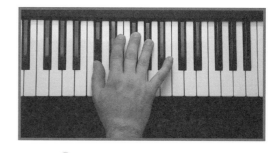

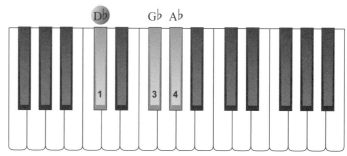

040

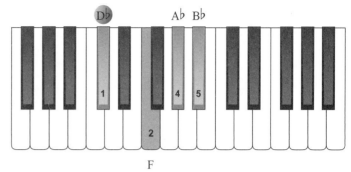

041

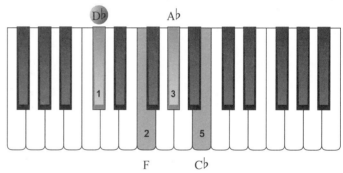

042

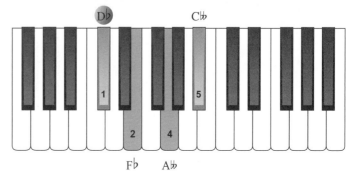

043

D♭maj⁷

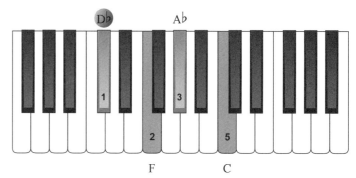

044

D♭m

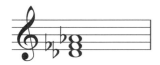

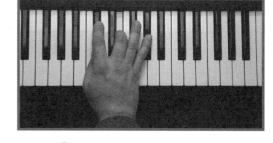

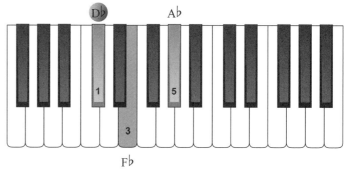

045

D♭m⁶

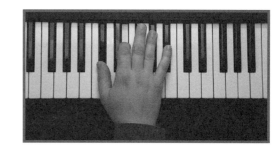

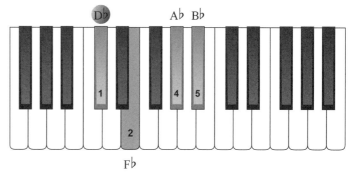

046

$D\flat m^7$

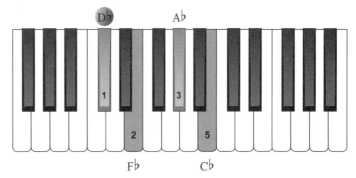

047

$D\flat m^{7\flat 5}$

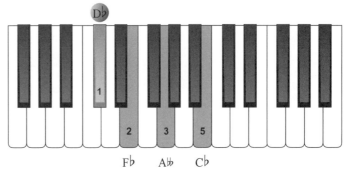

048

$D\flat^{7\flat 9}$

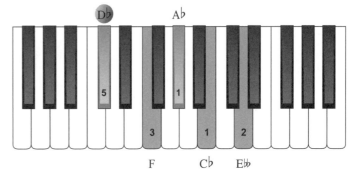

049

D♭7♯9

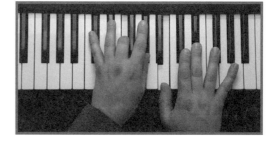

050

D♭9

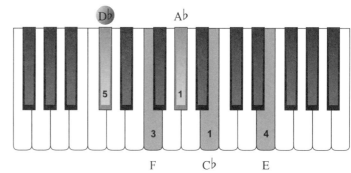

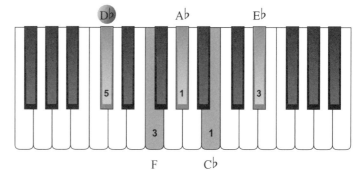

051

D♭9sus4

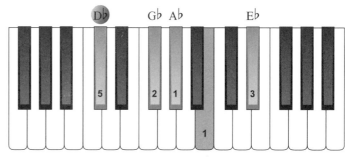

052

D♭9♭5

053

D♭9♯11

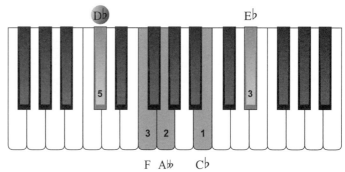

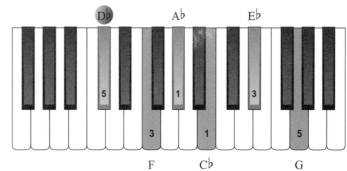

054

D♭13

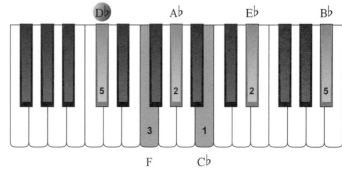

055

$D^{\flat}13^{\flat}5$

056

$D^{\flat}13^{\flat}9$

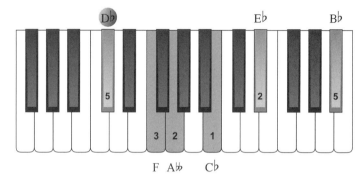

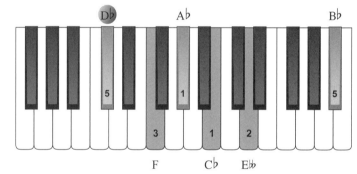

057

$D^{\flat}13^{\sharp}9$

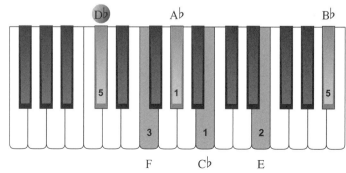

058

D♭13♭5♭9

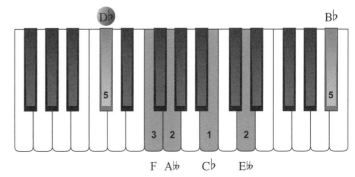

059

D♭13♭5♯9

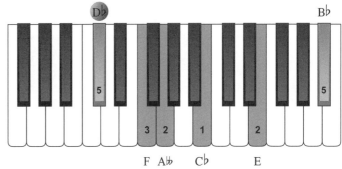

060

D♭13♯5♭9

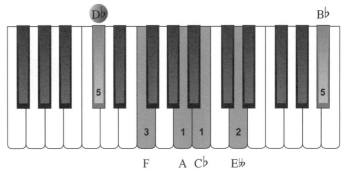

061

D♭13♯5♯9

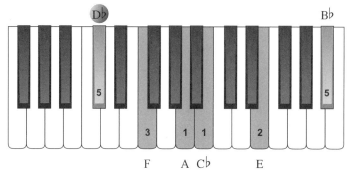

F   A   C♭   E

062

D♭6/9

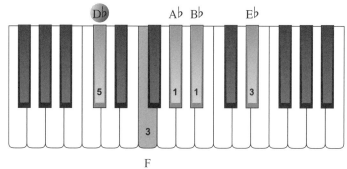

F

063

D♭maj9

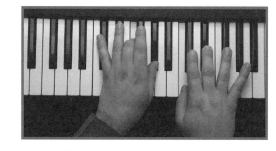

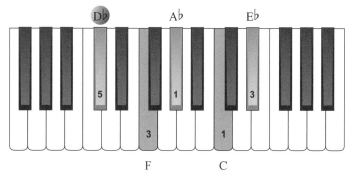

F   C

064

D♭maj⁹♯¹¹

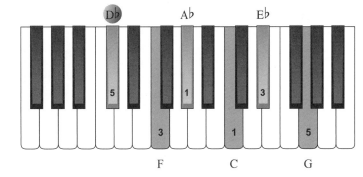

065

D♭maj¹³

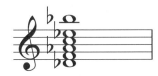

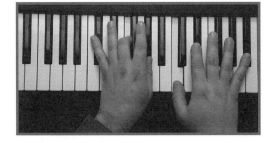

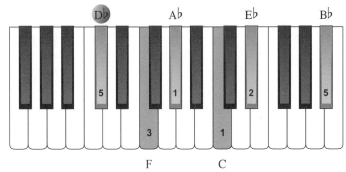

066

D♭maj¹³♭5

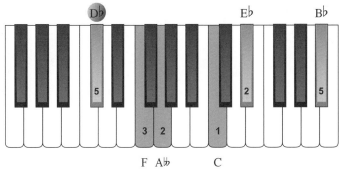

067

Dᵇmaj¹³♯5

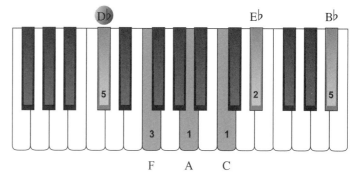

068

Dᵇmaj¹³ᵇ9

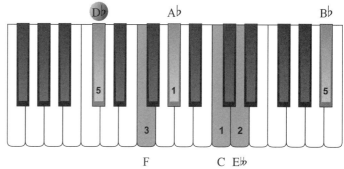

069

Dᵇmaj¹³♯9

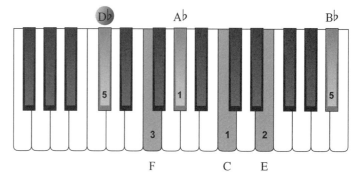

070

D♭m⁷♭⁹

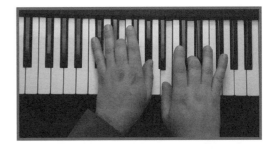

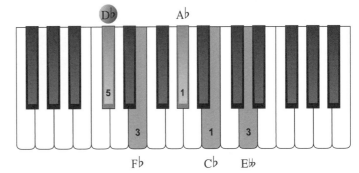

071

D♭m⁹

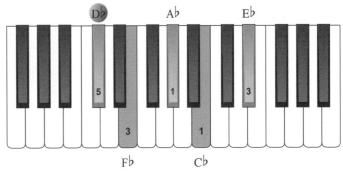

072

D♭m¹¹

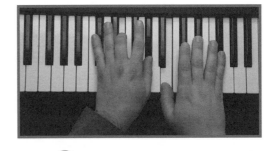

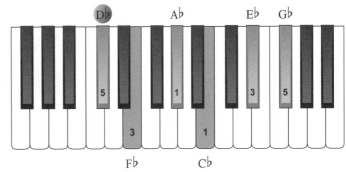

073

D

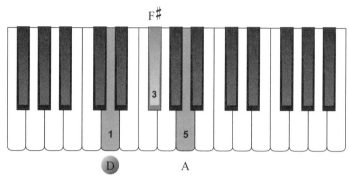

074

D+

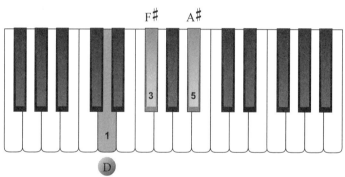

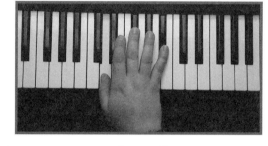

075

D^{SUS4}

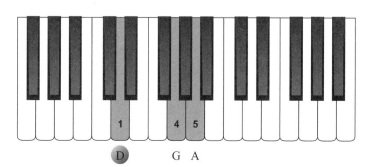

076

D⁶

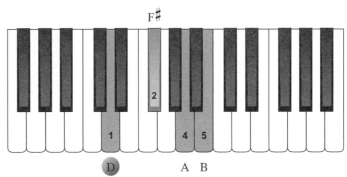

077

D⁷

078

Dᵒ⁷

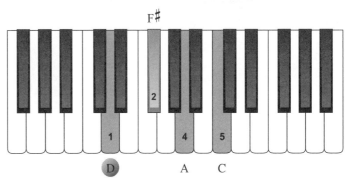

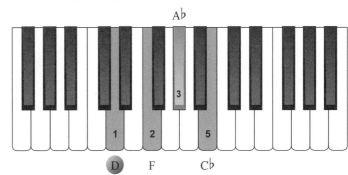

079

Dmaj⁷

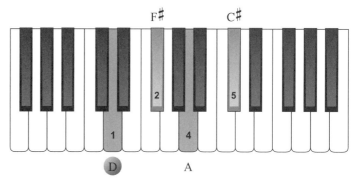

080

Dm

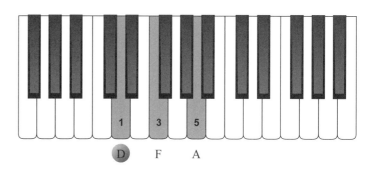

081

Dm⁶

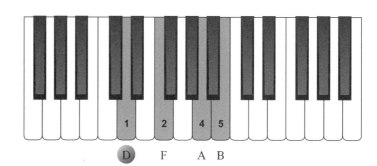

Dm⁷

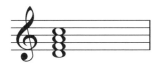

082

Dm^7

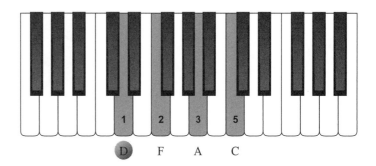

083

Dm^{7}$^\flat$^{5}

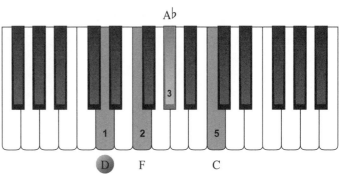

084

D^7$^\flat$^{9}

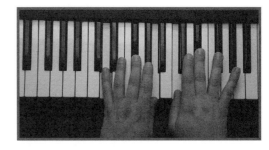

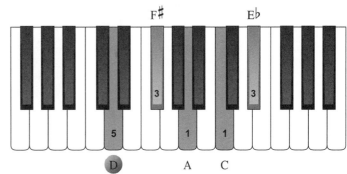

085

D^{7♯9}

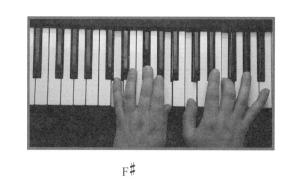

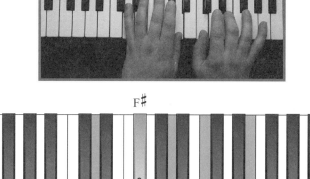

086

D⁹

087

D^{9sus4}

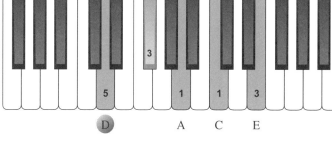

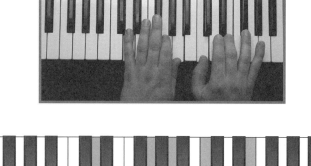

088

D⁹♭5

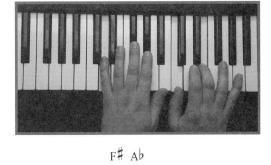
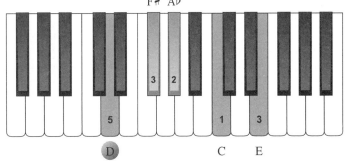

089

D⁹♯11

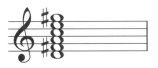

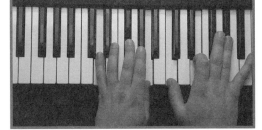
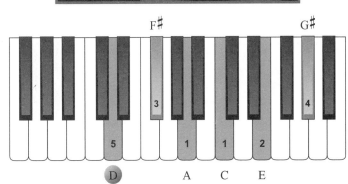

090

D¹³

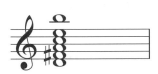

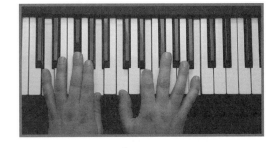
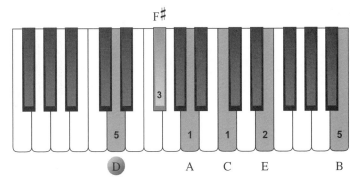

091

$D^{13\flat5}$

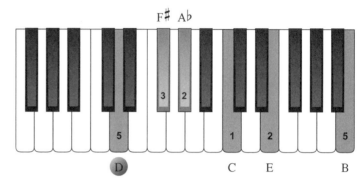

092

$D^{13\flat9}$

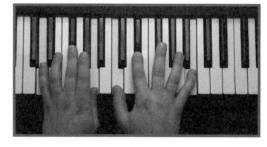

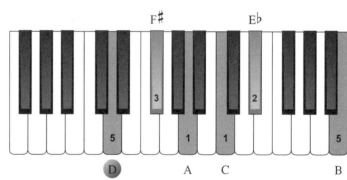

093

$D^{13\sharp9}$

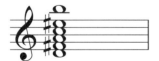

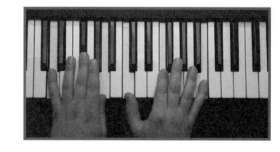

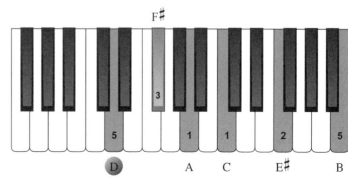

094

$D^{13\flat5\flat9}$

F♯ A♭   E♭

3 2   2

5   1   5

D   C   B

095

$D^{13\flat5\sharp9}$

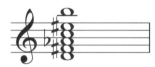

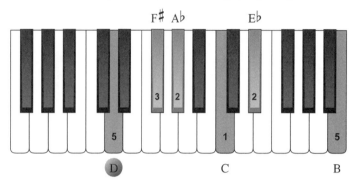

F♯ A♭

3 2

5   1   3   5

D   C   E♯   B

096

$D^{13\sharp5\flat9}$

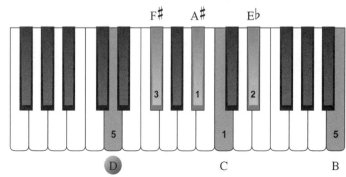

F♯   A♯   E♭

3   1   2

5   1   5

D   C   B

097

D^{13#5#9}

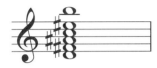

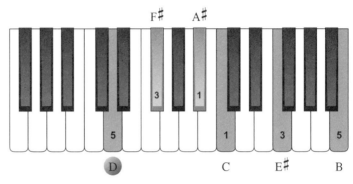

098

D^{6/9}

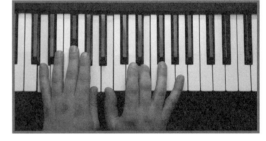

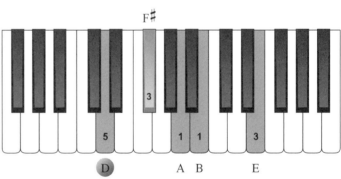

099

Dmaj⁹

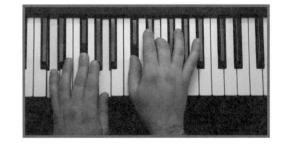

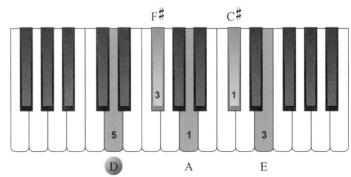

100

Dmaj⁹♯¹¹

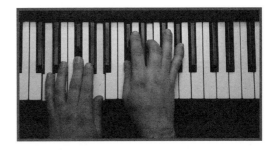

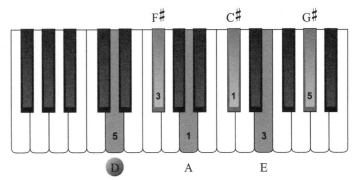

101

Dmaj¹³

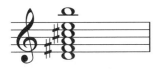

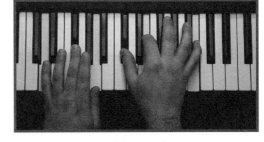

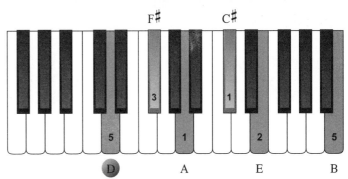

102

Dmaj¹³♭⁵

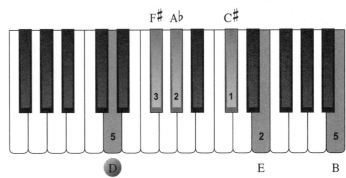

103

Dmaj^{13♯5}

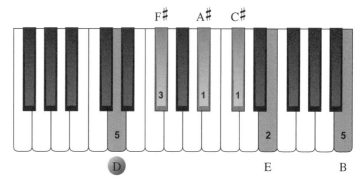

104

Dmaj^{13♭9}

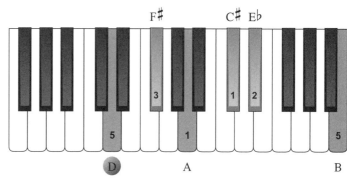

105

Dmaj^{13♯9}

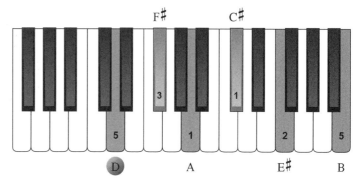

106

Dm$^{7\flat 9}$

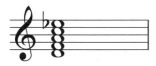

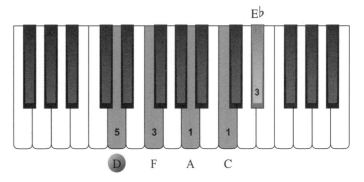

107

Dm^{9}

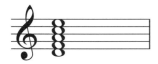

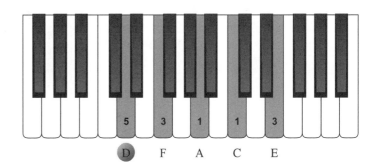

108

Dm^{11}

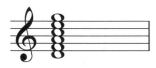

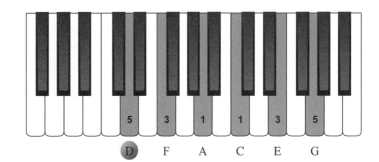

109

E♭

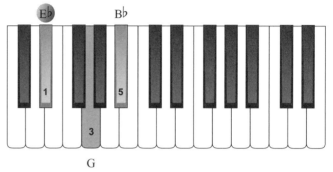

110

E♭+

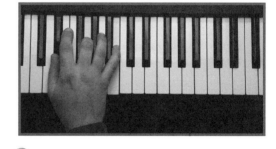

111

E♭sus4

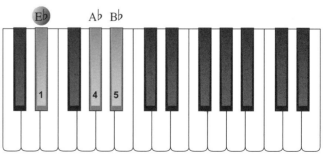

112

E$^{\flat}$6

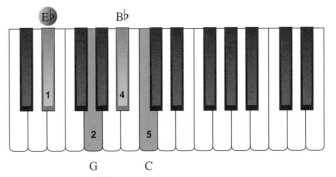

113

E$^{\flat}$7

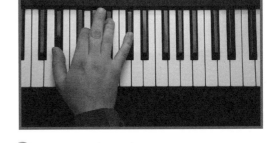

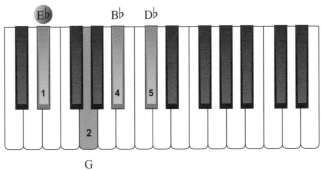

114

E$^{\flat}$o7

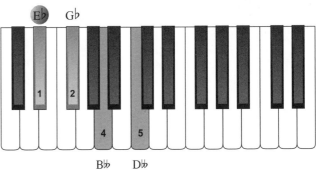

115

E♭maj⁷

116

E♭m

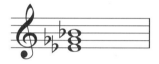

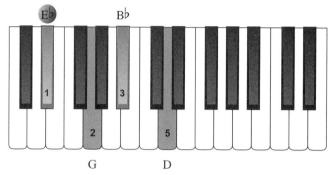

117

E♭m⁶

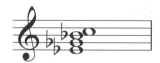

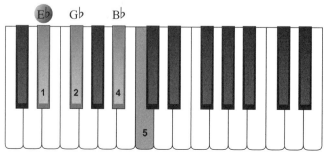

118

E♭m⁷

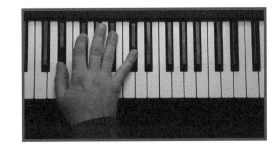

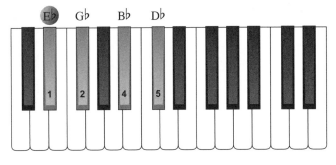

119

E♭m⁷♭5

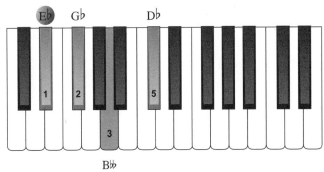

120

E♭7♭9

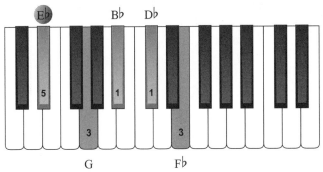

121

E♭7♯9

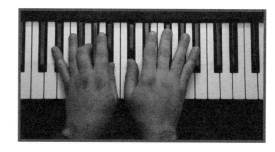

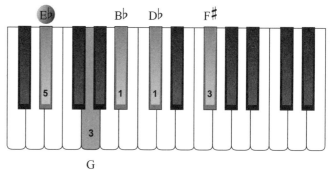

122

E♭9

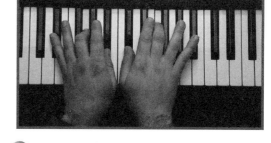

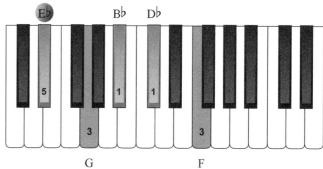

123

E♭9sus4

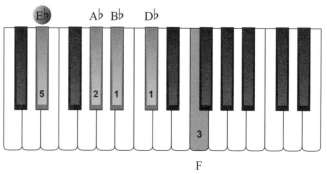

124

$E^{\flat 9 \flat 5}$

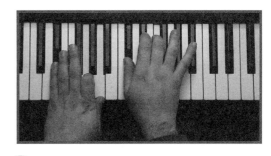
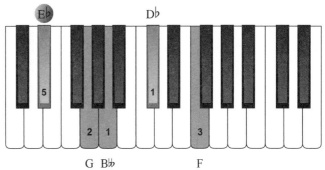

125

$E^{\flat 9 \sharp 11}$

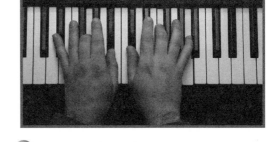
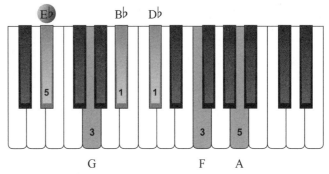

126

$E^{\flat 13}$

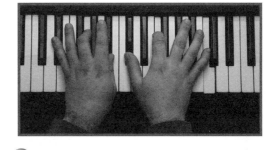
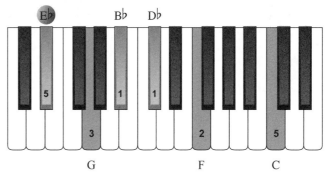

127

E♭13♭5

128

E♭13♭9

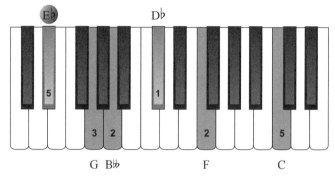

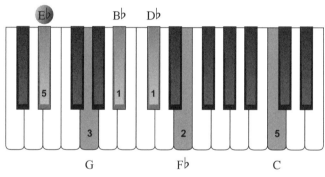

129

E♭13♯9

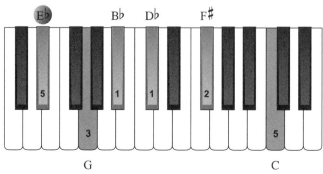

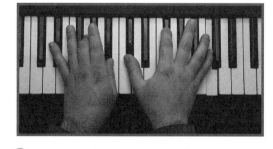

130

E♭13♭5♭9

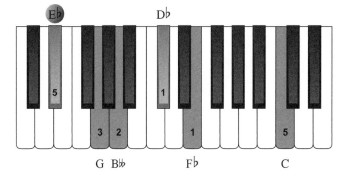

131

E♭13♭5♯9

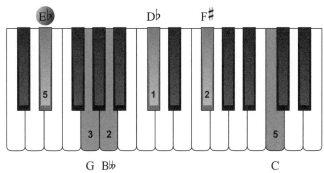

132

E♭13♯5♭9

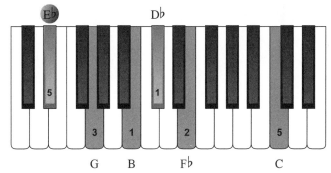

133

$E^{\flat}13\sharp5\sharp9$

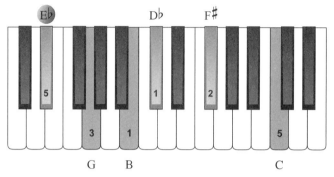

134

$E^{\flat}6/9$

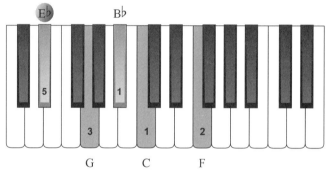

135

$E^{\flat}maj^{9}$

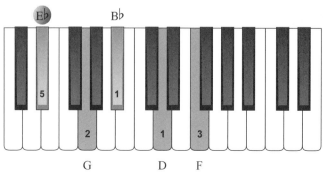

136

E♭maj⁹♯¹¹

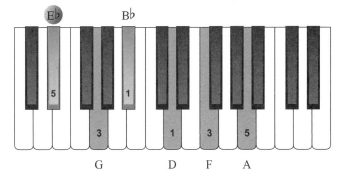

137

E♭maj¹³

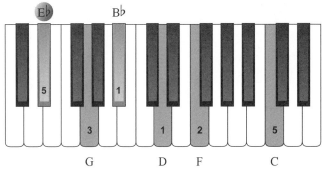

138

E♭maj¹³♭⁵

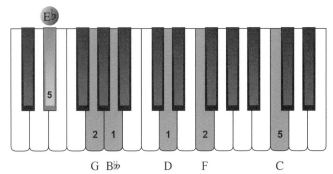

139

E♭maj¹³♯⁵

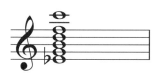

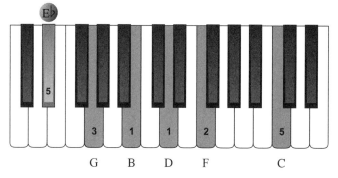

G B D F C

140

E♭maj¹³♭⁹

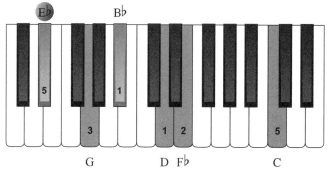

E♭ B♭

G D F♭ C

141

E♭maj¹³♯⁹

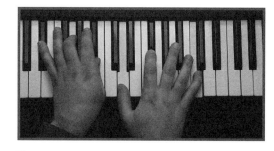

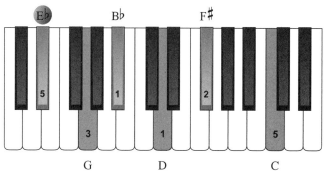

E♭ B♭ F♯

G D C

142

$E^\flat m^{7\flat 9}$

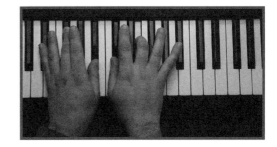

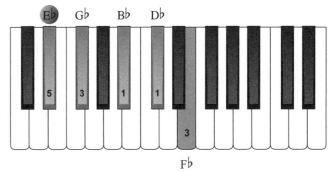

143

$E^\flat m^9$

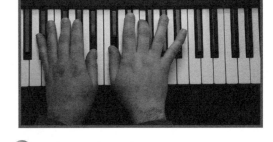

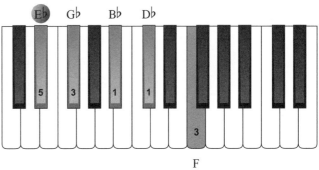

144

$E^\flat m^{11}$

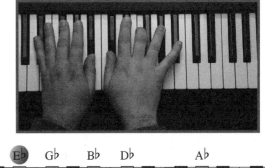

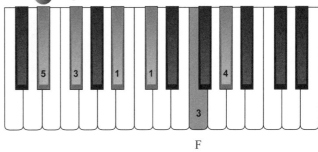

145

E

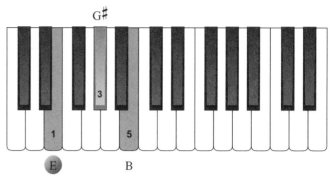

146

E+

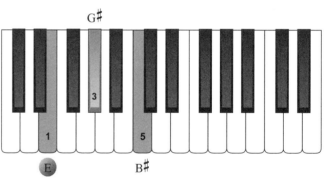

147

E SUS4

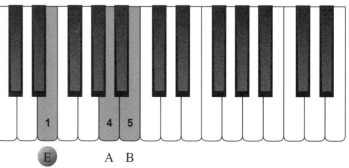

148

E⁶

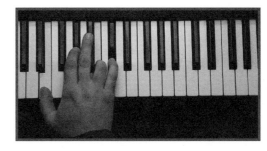

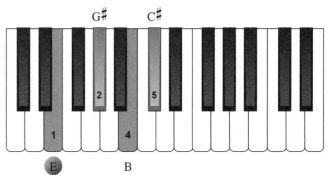

149

E⁷

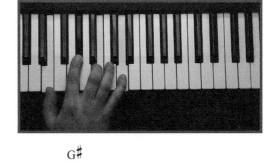

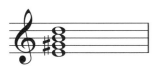

150

E°⁷

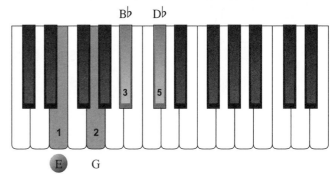

151

Emaj⁷

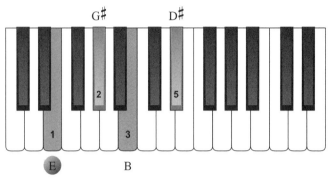

152

Em

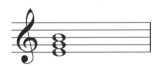

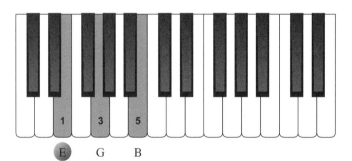

153

Em⁶

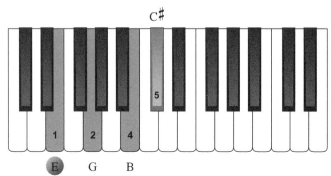

154

Em^7

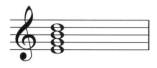

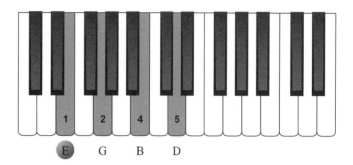

155

Em$^{7\flat5}$

156

E$^{7\flat9}$

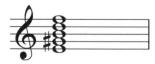

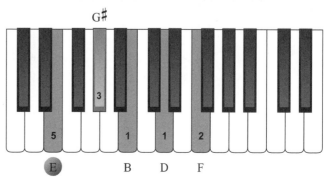

157

$E^{7\sharp9}$

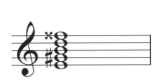

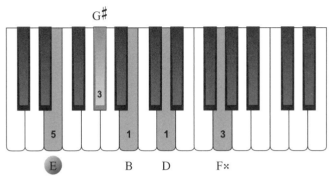

158

E^9

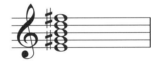

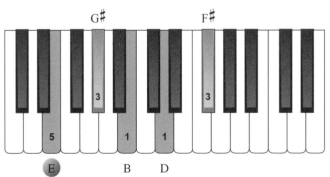

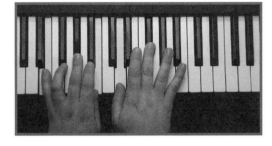

159

$E^{9}sus4$

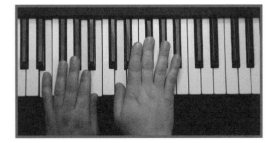

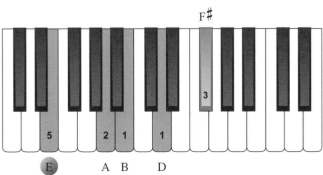

160

$E^{9\flat5}$

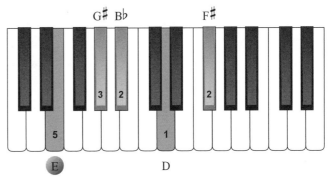

161

$E^{9\sharp11}$

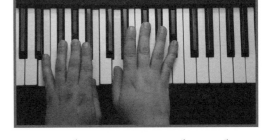

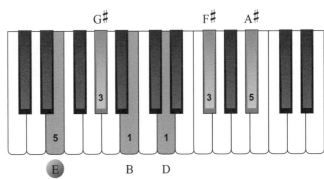

162

E^{13}

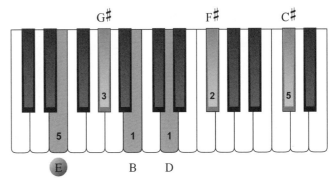

163

$E^{13\flat5}$

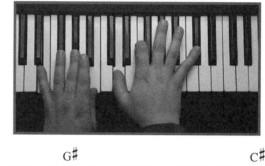

164

$E^{13\flat9}$

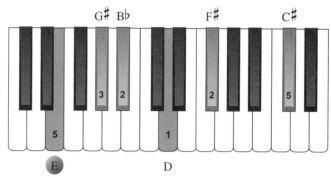

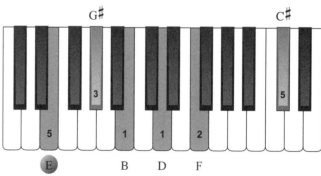

165

$E^{13\sharp9}$

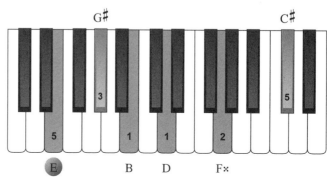

166

$E^{13\flat5\flat9}$

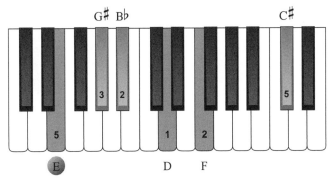

167

$E^{13\flat5\sharp9}$

168

$E^{13\sharp5\flat9}$

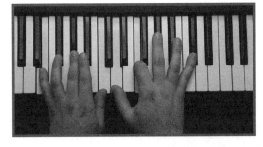

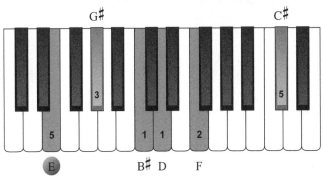

169

E¹³♯⁵♯⁹

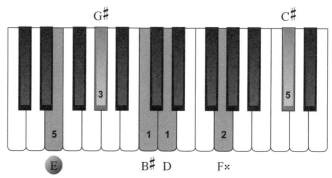

170

E⁶⁄₉

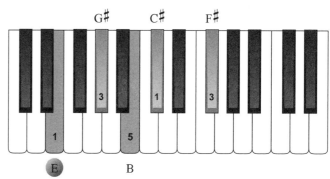

171

Emaj⁹

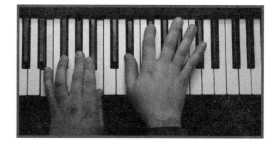

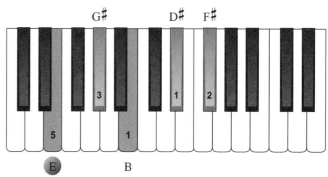

172

Emaj⁹♯11

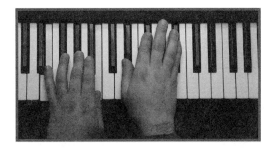

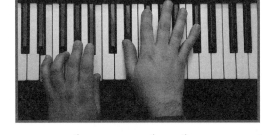

173

Emaj¹³

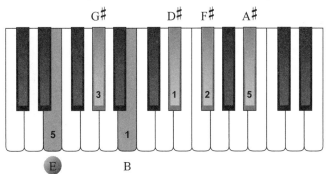

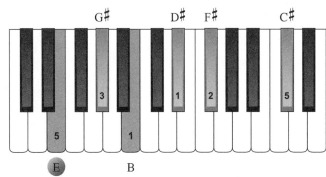

174

Emaj¹³♭⁵

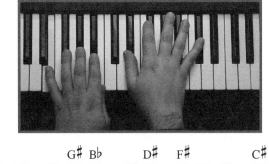

175

Emaj¹³♯5

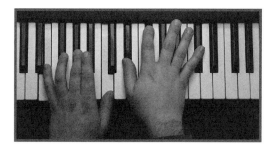

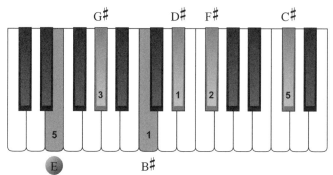

176

Emaj¹³♭9

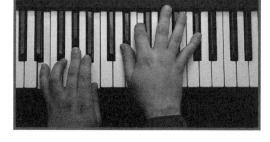

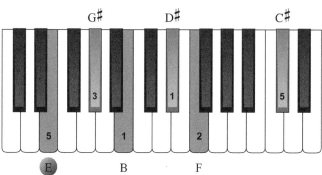

177

Emaj¹³♯9

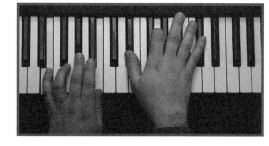

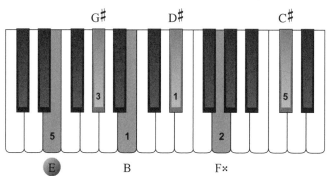

178

Em$^{7\flat9}$

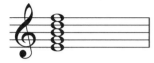

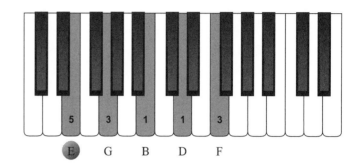

179

Em^{9}

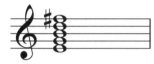

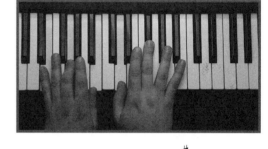

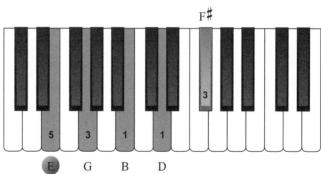

180

Em^{11}

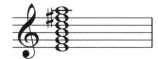

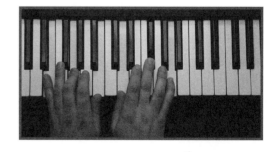

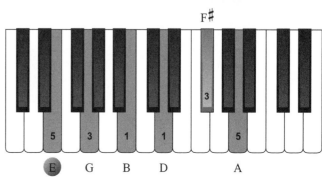

181

F

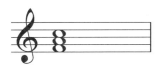

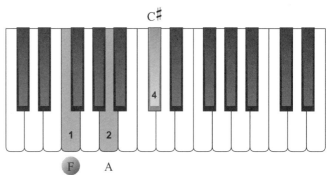

182

F+

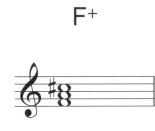

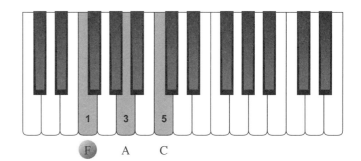

183

Fsus4

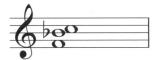

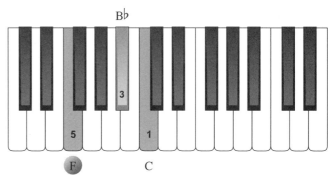

184

F⁶

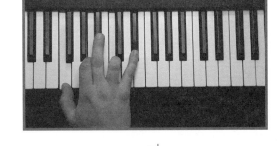

185

F⁷

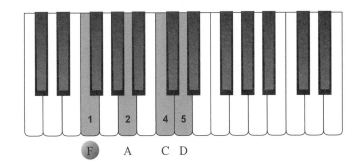

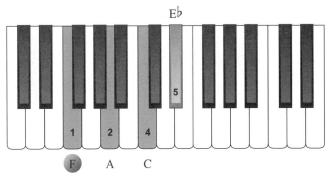

186

Fᴼ⁷

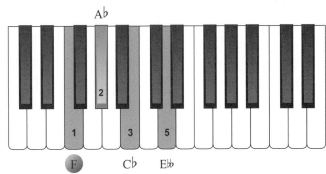

187

Fmaj⁷

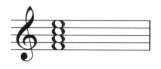

188

Fm

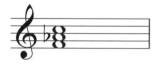

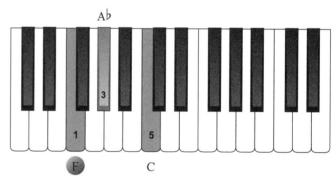

189

Fm⁶

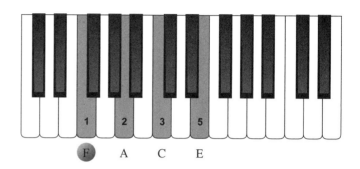

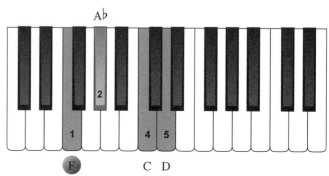

190

Fm⁷

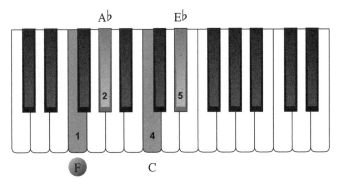

191

Fm⁷♭5

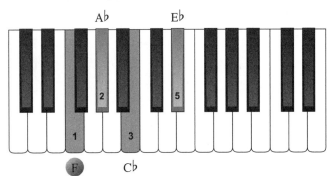

192

F⁷♭9

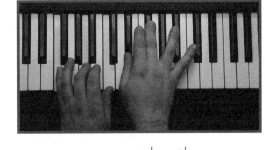

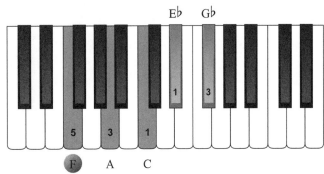

193

F⁷♯9

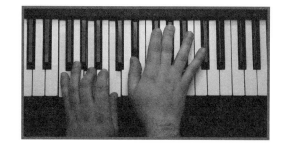

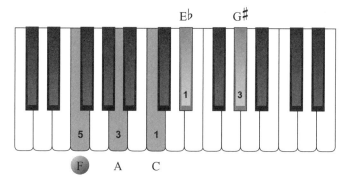

194

F⁹

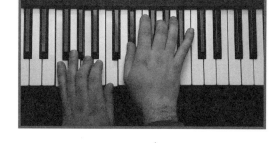

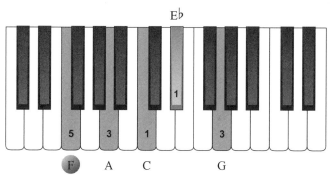

195

F⁹SUS4

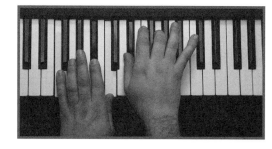

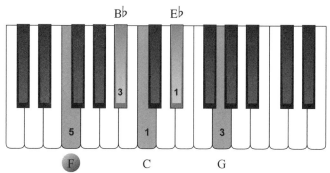

196

$F^{9\flat 5}$

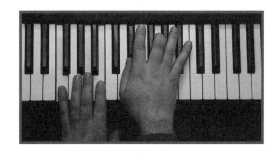

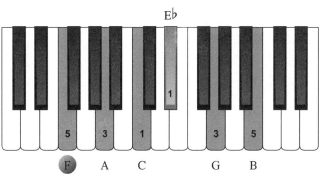

197

$F^{9\sharp 11}$

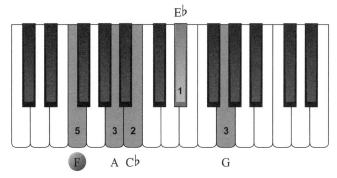

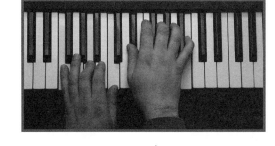

198

F^{13}

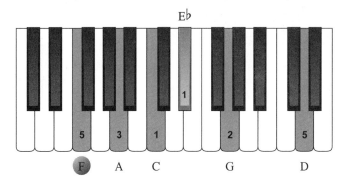

199

F¹³♭5

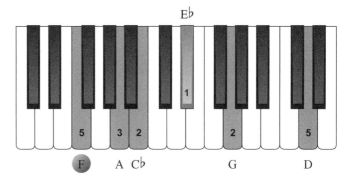

200

F¹³♭9

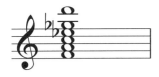

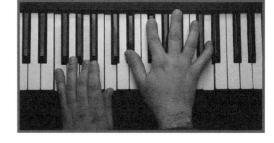

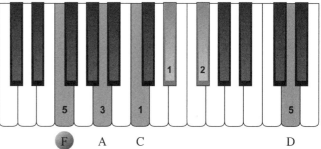

201

F¹³#9

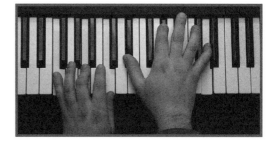

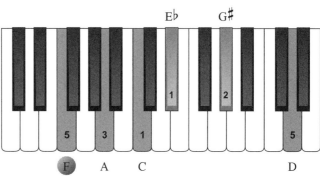

202

F¹³ᵇ⁵ᵇ⁹

203

F¹³ᵇ⁵#⁹

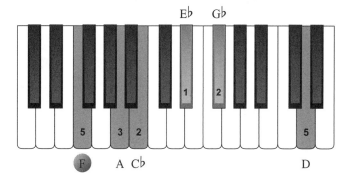

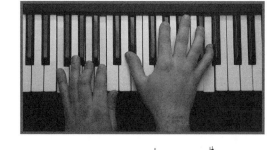

204

F¹³#⁵ᵇ⁹

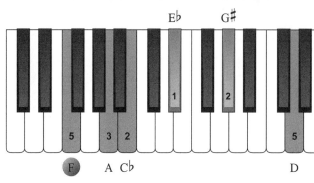

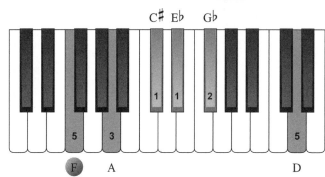

205

F¹³#⁵#⁹

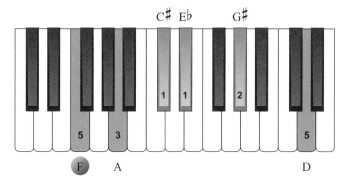

206

F⁶/₉

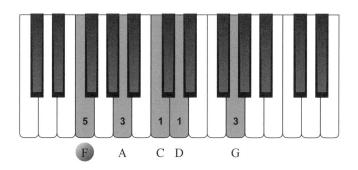

207

Fmaj⁹

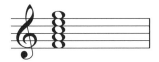

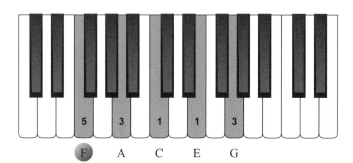

208

Fmaj^{9#11}

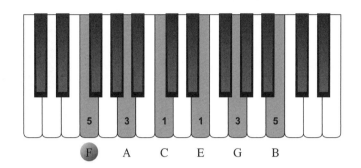

209

Fmaj¹³

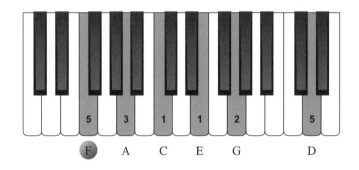

210

Fmaj^{13b5}

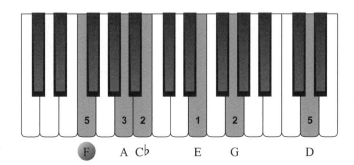

211

Fmaj^{13#5}

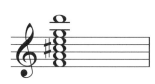

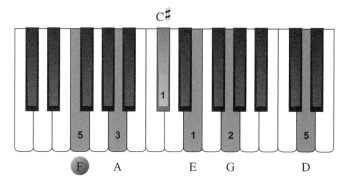

212

Fmaj^{13♭9}

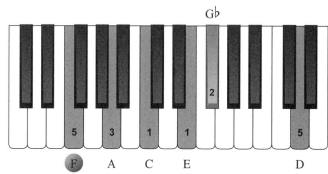

213

Fmaj^{13#9}

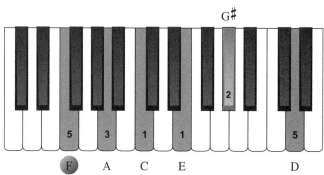

214

Fm^{7♭9}

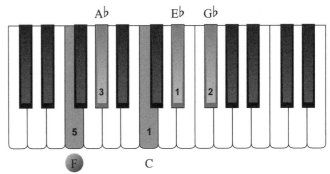

215

Fm⁹

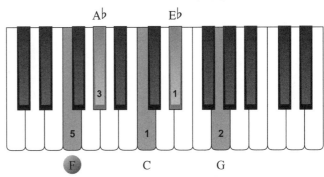

216

Fm¹¹

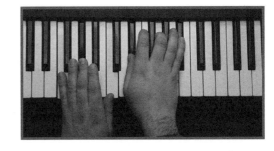

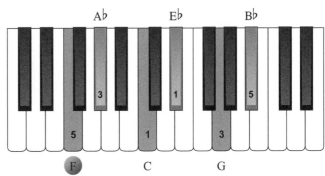

001

F#

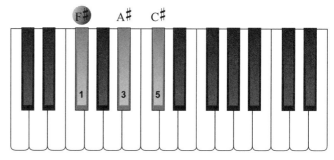

002

F#+

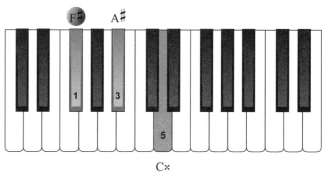

003

F#sus4

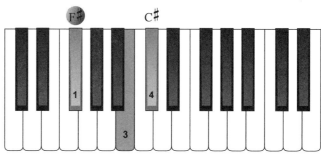

004

F#6

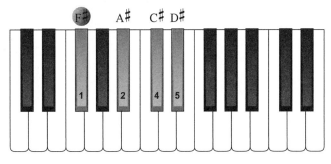

005

F#7

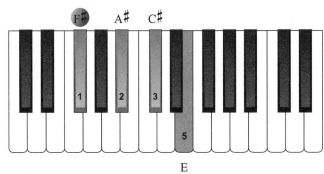

006

F#o7

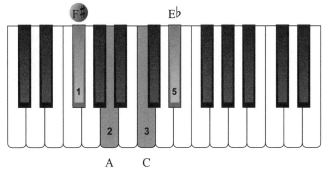

007

F#maj⁷

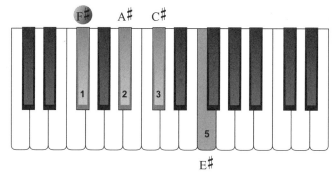

008

F#m

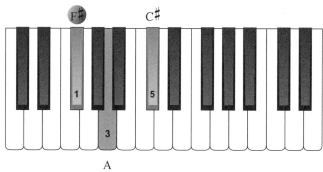

009

F#m⁶

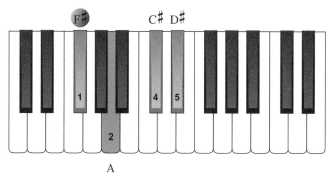

010

F#m⁷

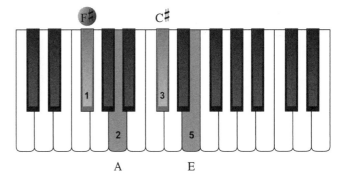

011

F#m⁷♭5

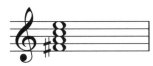

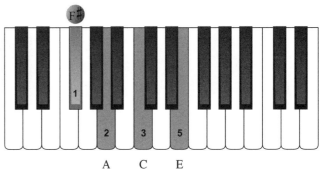

012

F#7♭9

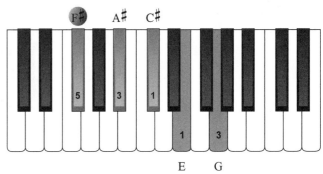

013

F#7#9

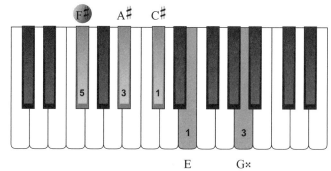

014

F#9

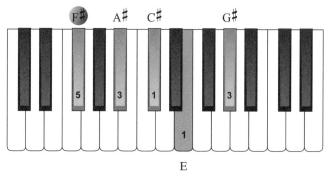

015

F#9sus4

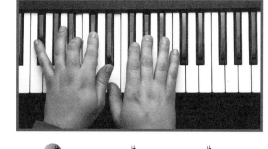

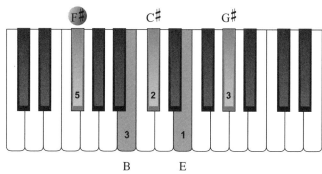

016

F#9♭5

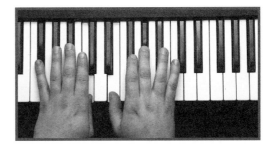

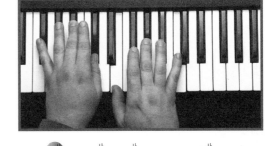

017

F#9#11

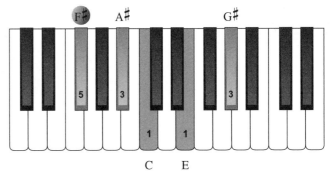

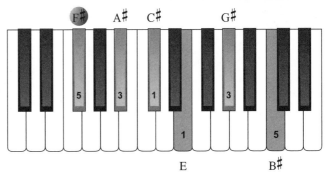

018

F#13

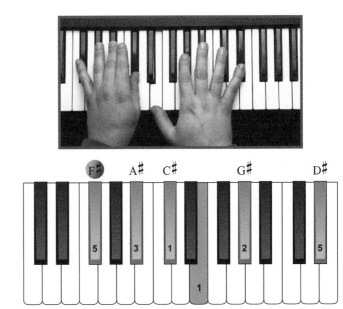

019

F#13♭5

020

F#13♭9

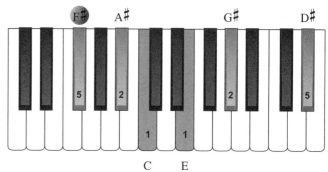

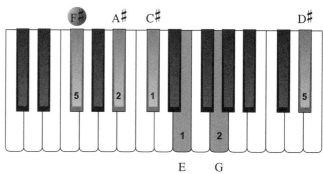

021

F#13#9

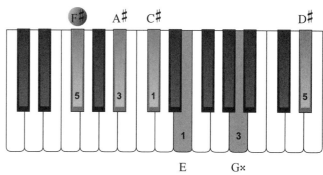

022

F#13♭5♭9

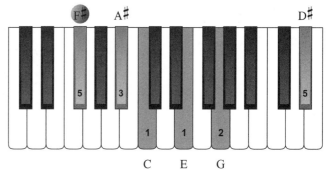

023

F#13♭5#9

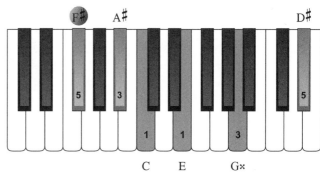

024

F#13#5♭9

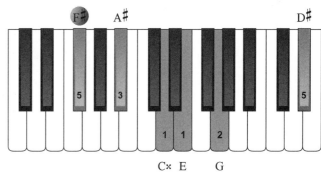

025

F#13#5#9

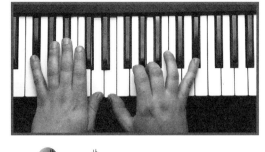

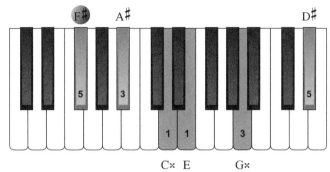

026

F#6/9

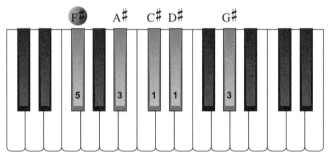

027

F#maj⁹

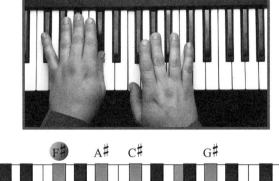

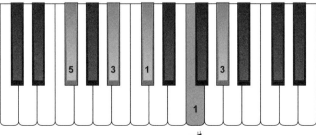

028

F#maj⁹#11

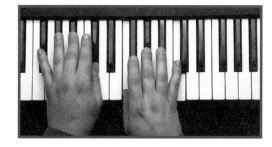

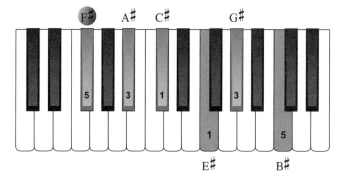

029

F#maj¹³

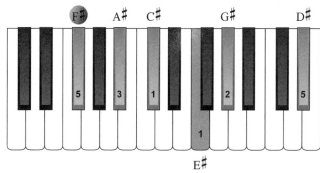

030

F#maj¹³♭5

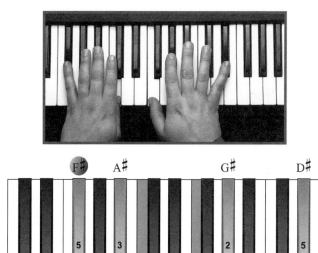

031

F#maj¹³#5

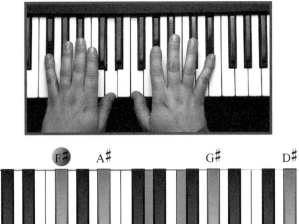

032

F#maj¹³♭9

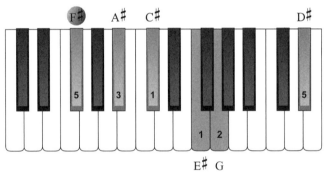

033

F#maj¹³#9

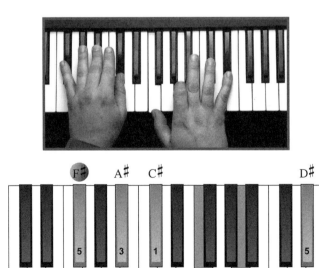

034

F#m⁷♭⁹

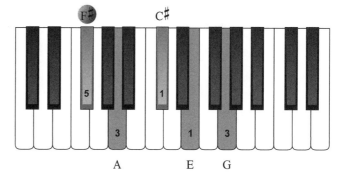

035

F#m⁹

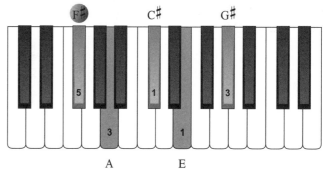

036

F#m¹¹

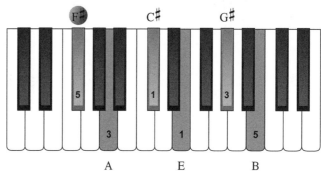

037

G

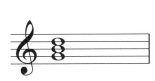

1 3 5
G B D

038

G⁺

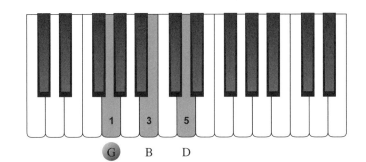

D#

5

1 2
G B

039

G^{SUS4}

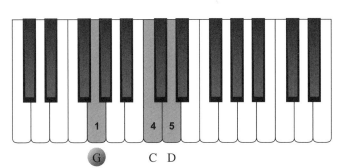

1 4 5
G C D

040

G⁶

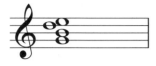

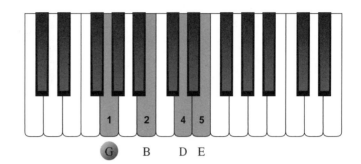

041

G⁷

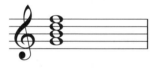

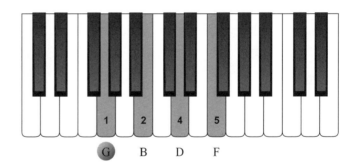

042

Gᴼ⁷

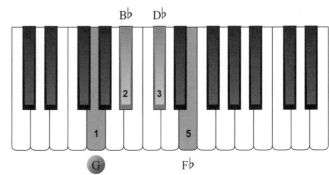

043

Gmaj⁷

F#

5

1   2   3

G   B   D

044

Gm

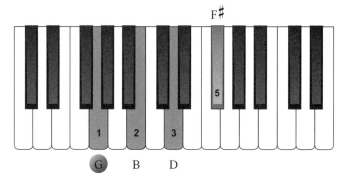

B♭

3

1   5

G   D

045

Gm⁶

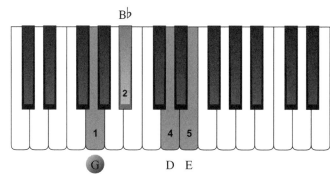

B♭

2

1   4 5

G   D E

046

Gm⁷

047

Gm⁷♭⁵

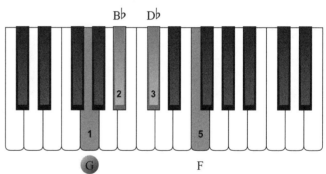

048

G⁷♭⁹

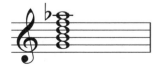

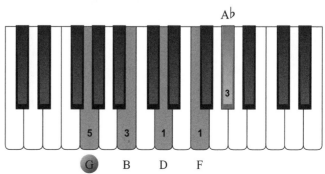

049

G⁷#9

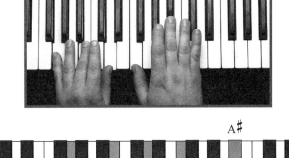

A#

5 3 1 1 3
G B D F

050

G⁹

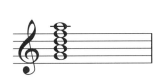

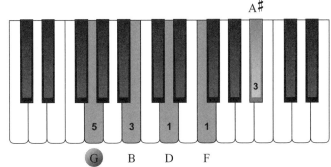

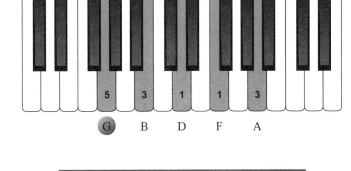

5 3 1 1 3
G B D F A

051

G⁹SUS4

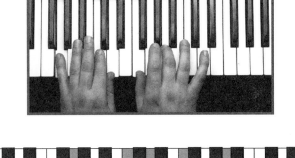

5 2 1 1 3
G C D F A

052

G⁹♭5

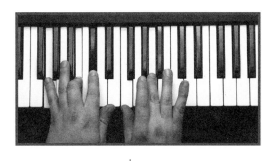

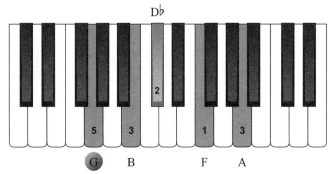

053

G⁹♯11

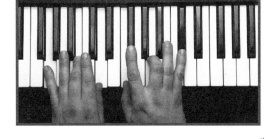

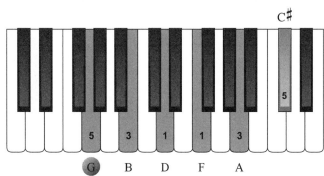

054

G¹³

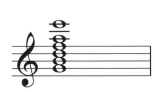

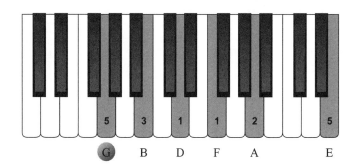

055

G$^{13\flat5}$

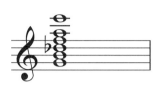

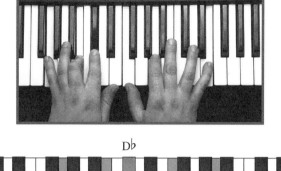

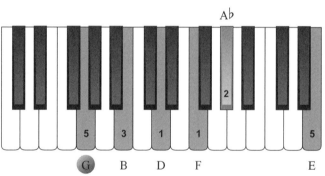

Db

| 5 | 3 | | 1 | 2 | 5 |
| G | B | | F | A | E |

056

G$^{13\flat9}$

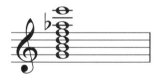

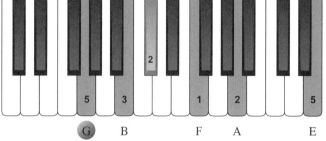

Ab

| 5 | 3 | 1 | 1 | 2 | 5 |
| G | B | D | F | | E |

057

G$^{13\sharp9}$

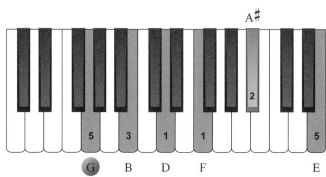

A#

| 5 | 3 | 1 | 1 | 2 | 5 |
| G | B | D | F | | E |

058

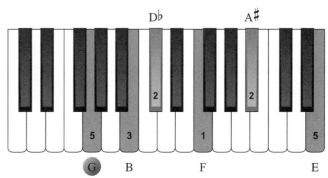

059

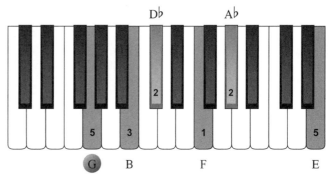

060

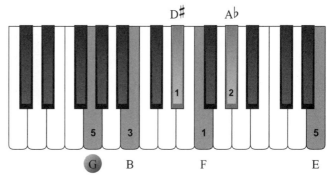

061

G¹³#5#9

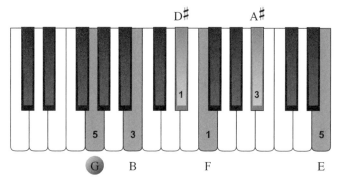

062

G⁶⁄₉

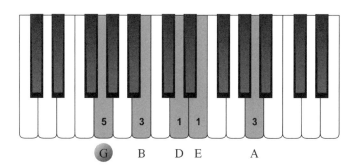

063

Gmaj⁹

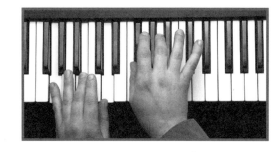

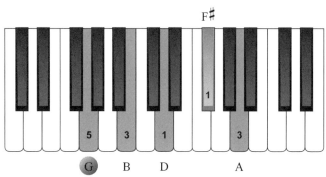

064

Gmaj⁹♯11

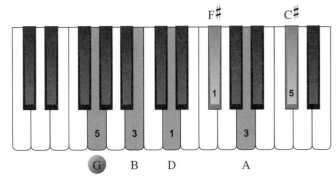

065

Gmaj¹³

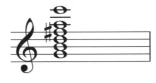

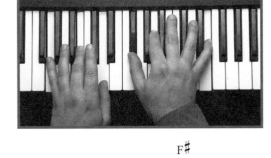

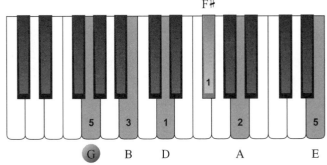

066

Gmaj¹³♭5

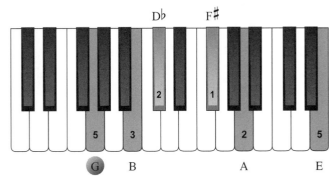

067

Gmaj¹³♯⁵

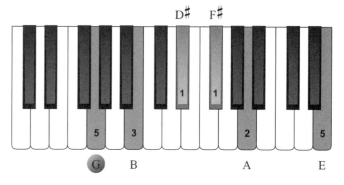

068

Gmaj¹³♭⁹

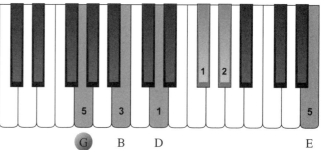

069

Gmaj¹³♯⁹

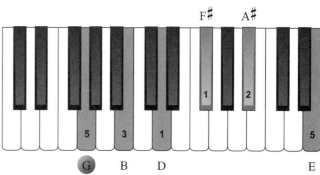

070

Gm⁷♭⁹

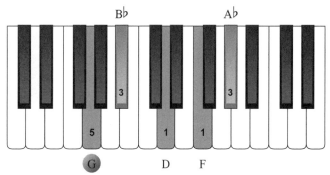

071

Gm⁹

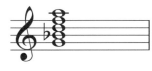

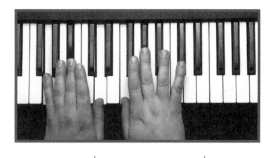

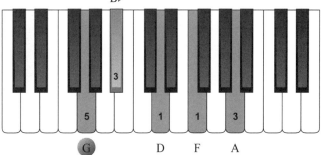

072

Gm¹¹

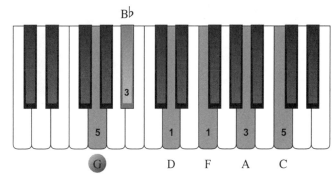

073

A♭

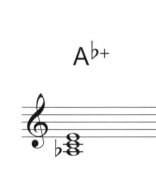

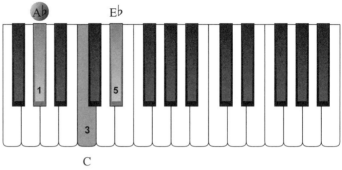

074

A♭+

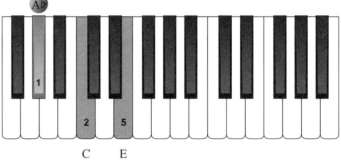

075

A♭sus4

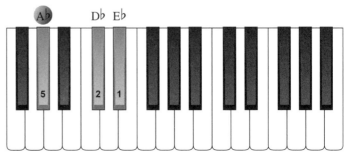

076

A♭6

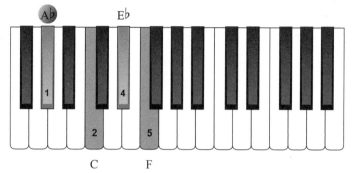

077

A♭7

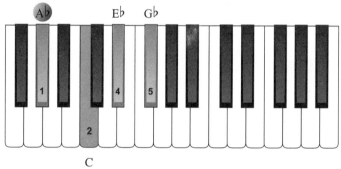

078

A♭o7

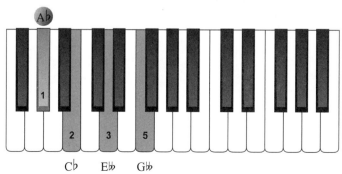

079

A♭maj⁷

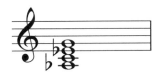

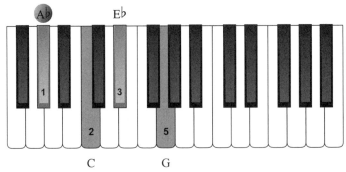

Ab   Eb

1   3

2   5

C   G

080

A♭m

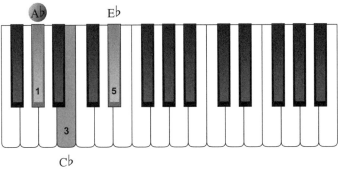

Ab   Eb

1   5

3

C♭

081

A♭m⁶

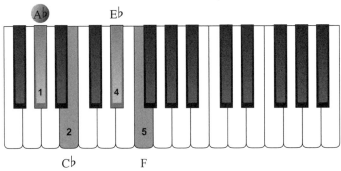

Ab   Eb

1   4

2   5

C♭   F

082

A♭m⁷

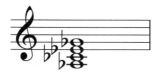

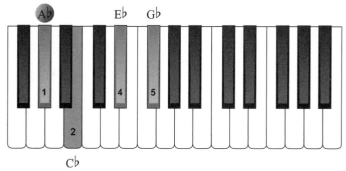

083

A♭m⁷♭5

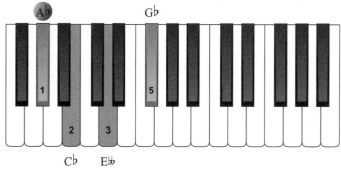

084

A♭7♭9

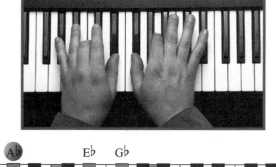

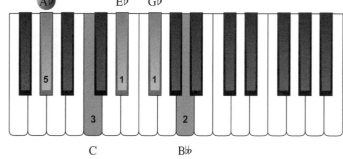

085

A♭7♯9

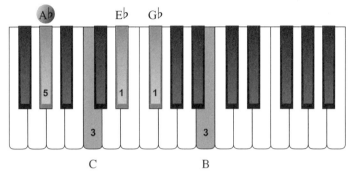

086

A♭9

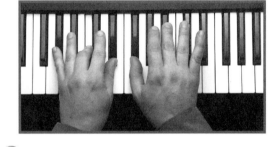

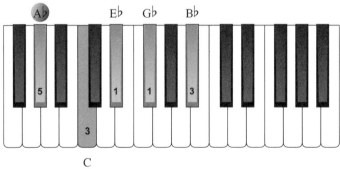

087

A♭9sus4

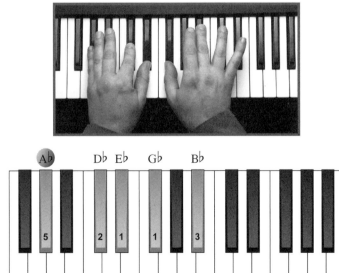

088

A♭9♭5

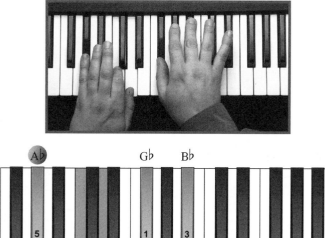

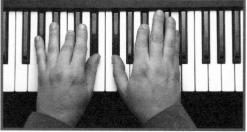

089

A♭9♯11

090

A♭13

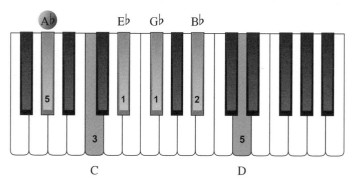

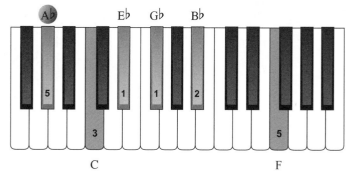

091

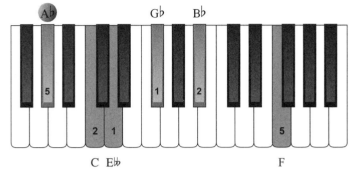

092

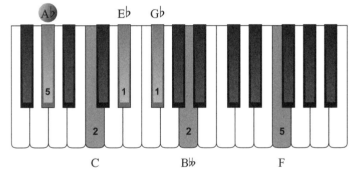

093

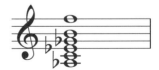

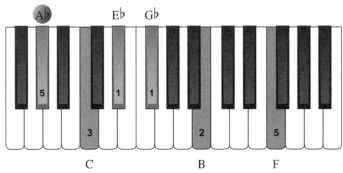

094

A♭13♭5♭9

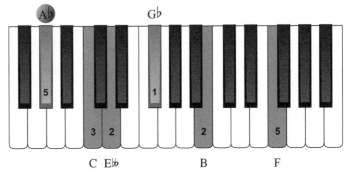

095

A♭13♭5♯9

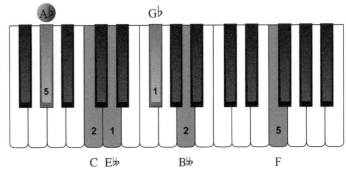

096

A♭13♯5♭9

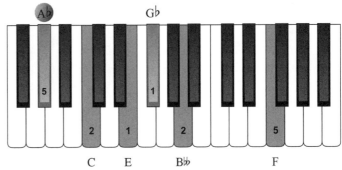

097

A♭13#5#9

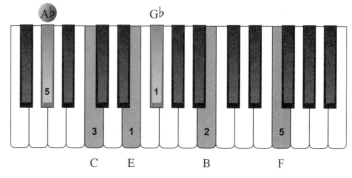

098

A♭6/9

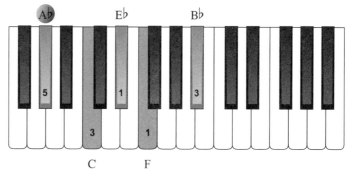

099

A♭maj9

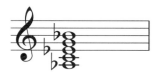

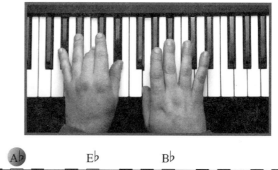

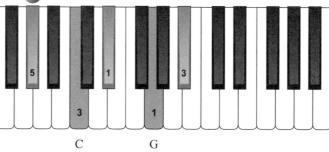

100

A♭maj⁹♯¹¹

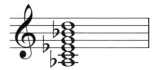

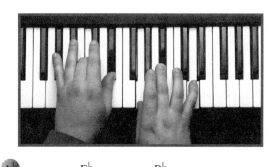

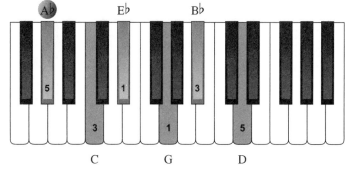

101

A♭maj¹³

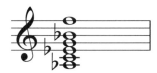

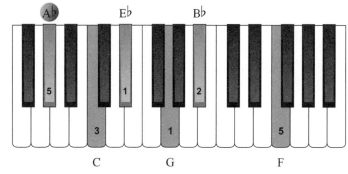

102

A♭maj¹³♭5

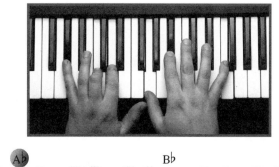

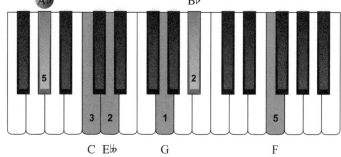

103

A♭maj¹³♯5

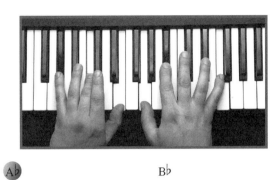

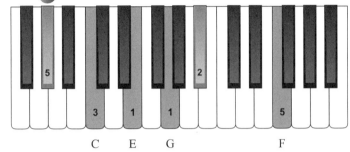

104

A♭maj¹³♭9

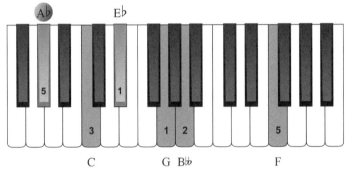

105

A♭maj¹³♯9

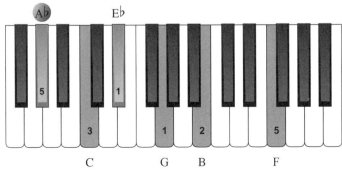

106

$A^\flat m^{7\flat 9}$

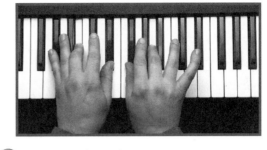

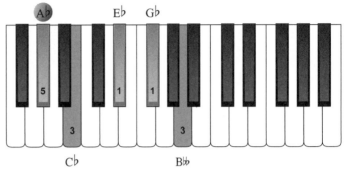

107

$A^\flat m^9$

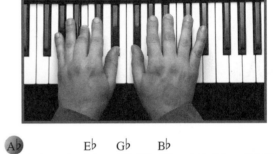

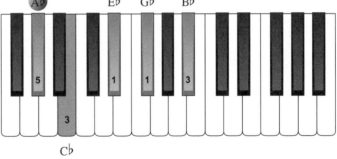

108

$A^\flat m^{11}$

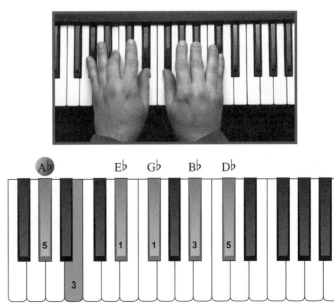

109

A

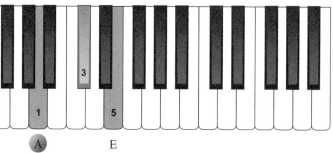

110

A⁺

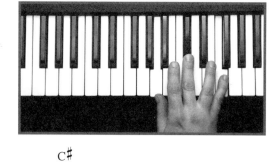

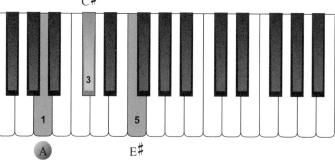

111

Aˢᵘˢ4

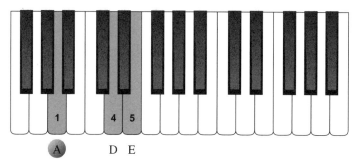

112

A⁶

113

A⁷

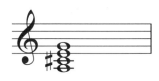

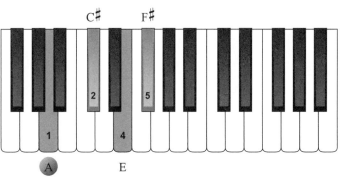

114

Aᵒ⁷

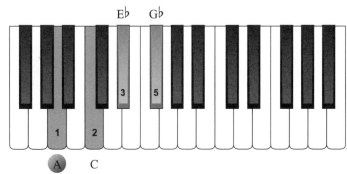

115

Amaj⁷

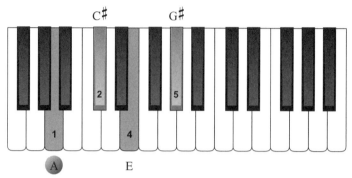

116

Am

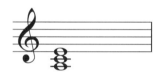

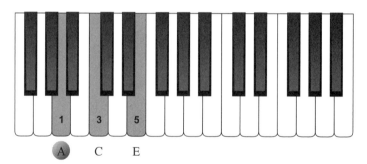

117

Am⁶

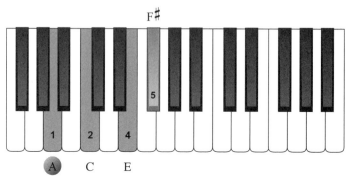

118

Am⁷

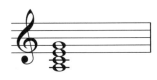

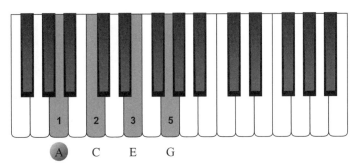

119

Am⁷♭5

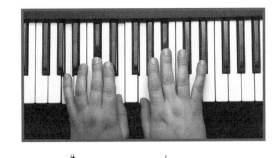

120

A⁷♭9

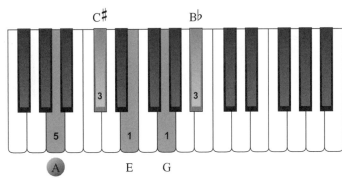

121

A⁷**9**

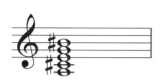

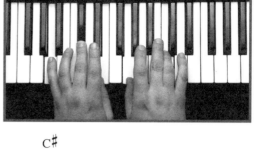

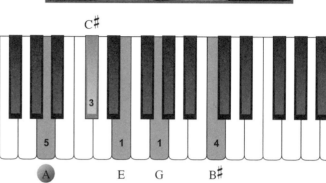

122

A⁹

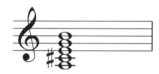

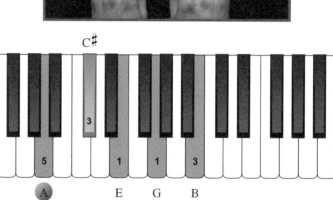

123

A⁹SUS4

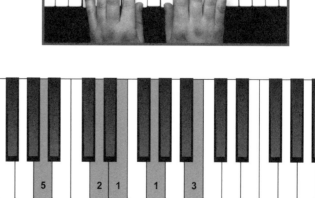

124

A⁹♭5

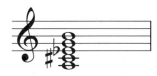

125

A⁹♯11

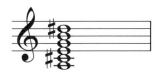

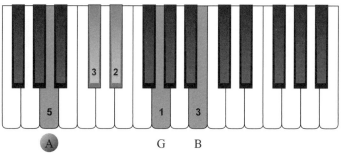

126

A¹³

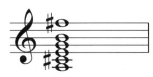

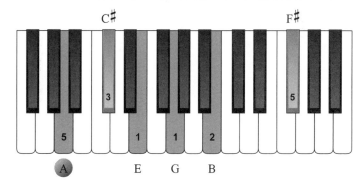

127

A^{13♭5}

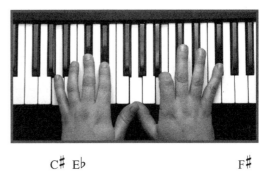

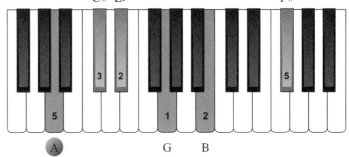

128

A^{13♭9}

129

A^{13♯9}

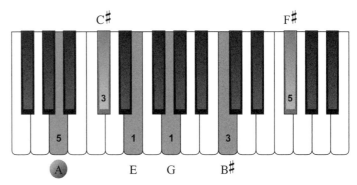

130

A$^{13♭5♭9}$

131

A$^{13♭5♯9}$

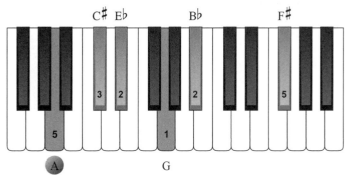

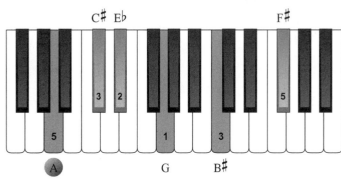

132

A$^{13♯5♭9}$

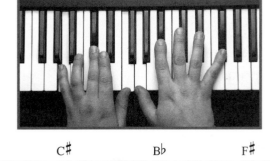

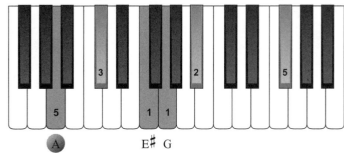

133

A¹³♯⁵♯⁹

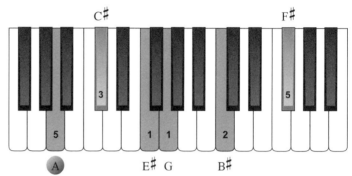

134

A⁶⁄₉

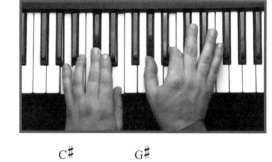

135

Amaj⁹

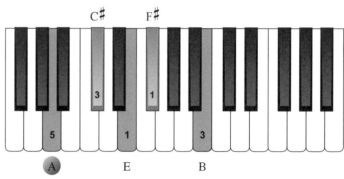

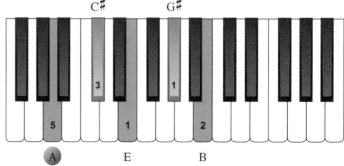

136

Amaj⁹♯¹¹

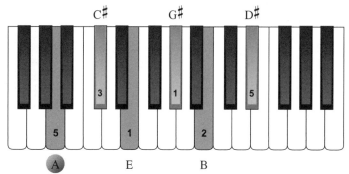

137

Amaj¹³

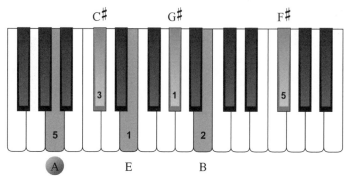

138

Amaj¹³♭⁵

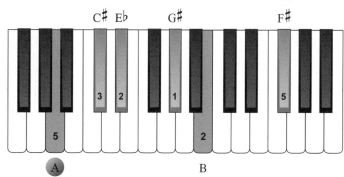

139

Amaj^{13♯5}

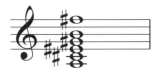

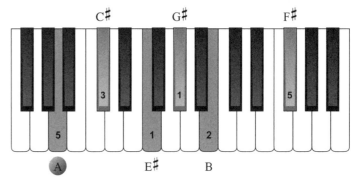

140

Amaj^{13♭9}

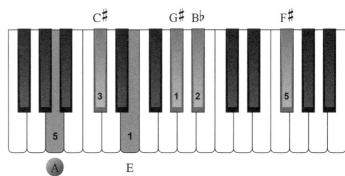

141

Amaj^{13♯9}

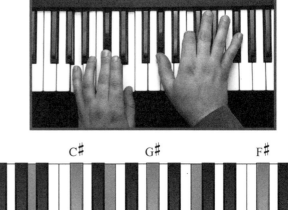

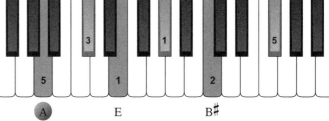

142

Am⁷♭⁹

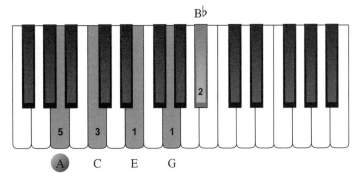

143

Am⁹

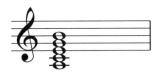

144

Am¹¹

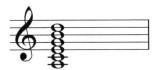

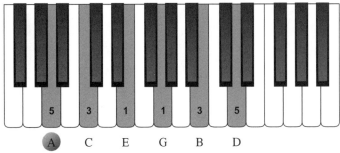

145

B♭

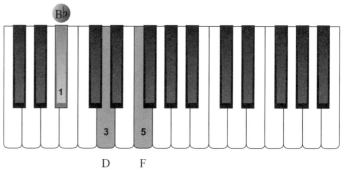

D   F

146

B♭+

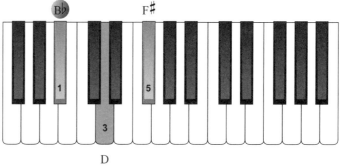

B♭   F♯

D

147

B♭sus4

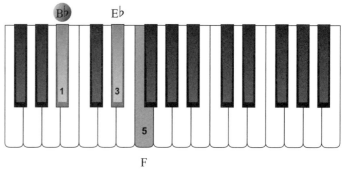

B♭   E♭

F

148

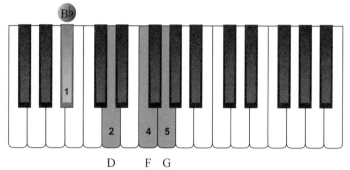

149

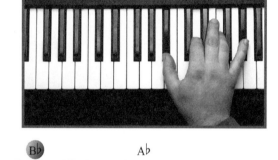

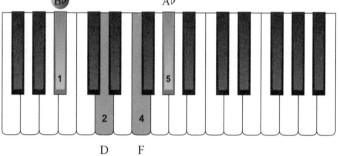

150

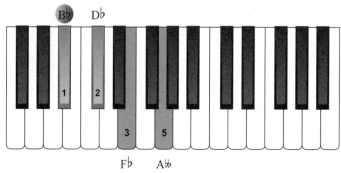

151

B♭maj⁷

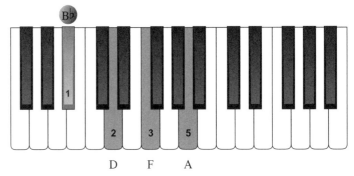

D   F   A

152

B♭m

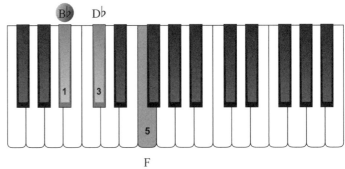

F

153

B♭m⁶

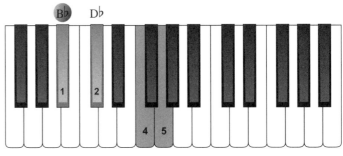

F G

154

$B\flat m^7$

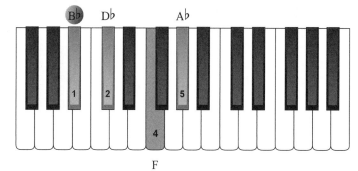

155

$B\flat m^{7\flat 5}$

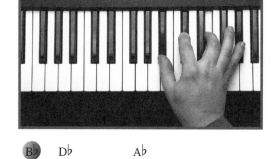

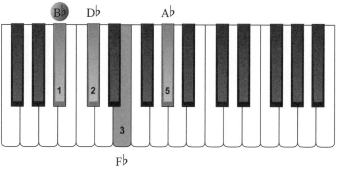

156

$B\flat^{7\flat 9}$

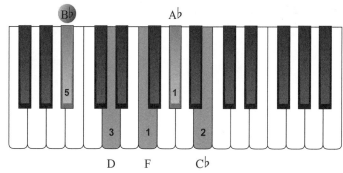

157

$B^{\flat 7\sharp 9}$

158

$B^{\flat 9}$

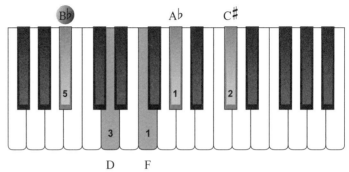

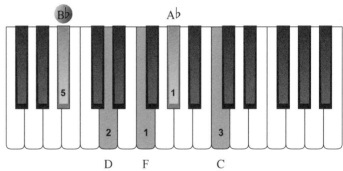

159

$B^{\flat 9}sus4$

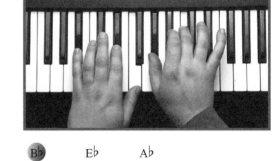

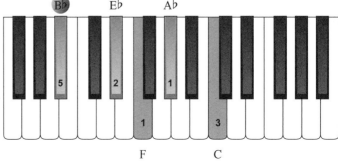

160

B♭9♭5

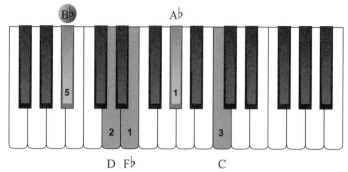

161

B♭9♯11

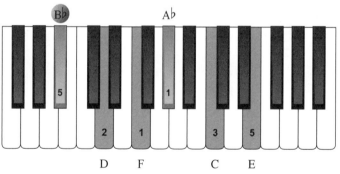

162

B♭13

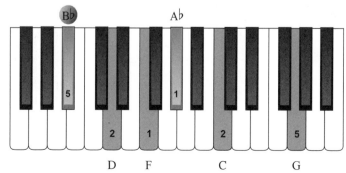

163

B♭13♭5

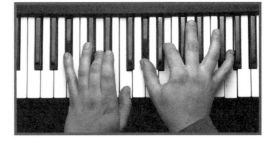

164

B♭13♭9

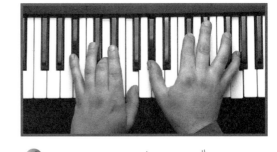

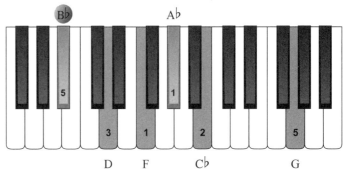

165

B♭13♯9

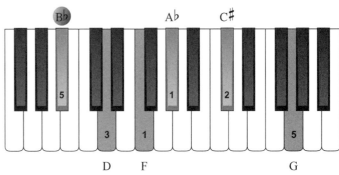

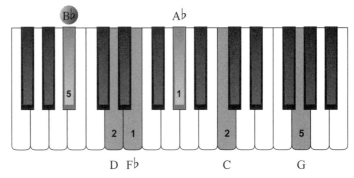

166

B♭13♭5♭9

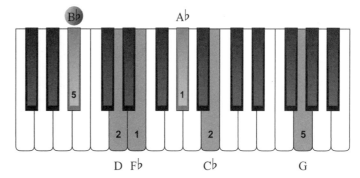

167

B♭13♭5♯9

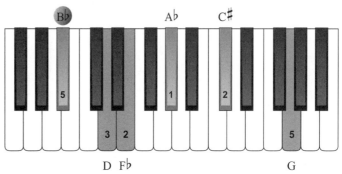

168

B♭13♯5♭9

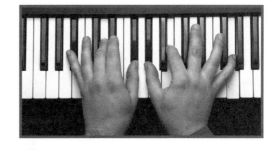

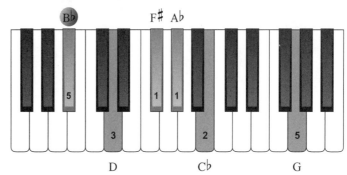

169

B♭13#5#9

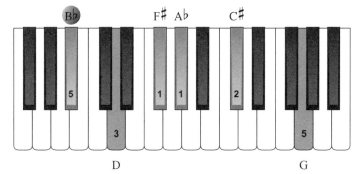

F# A♭   C#

B♭

5   3   1 1   2   5

D   G

170

B♭6/9

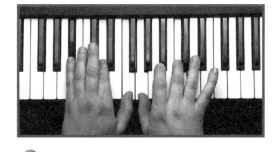

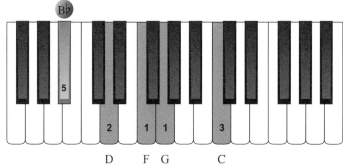

B♭

5   2 1 1   3

D F G   C

171

B♭maj9

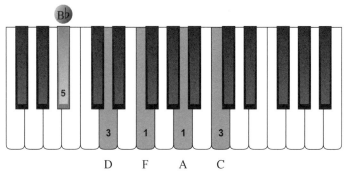

B♭

5   3 1   1   3

D F   A   C

172

B♭maj⁹♯¹¹

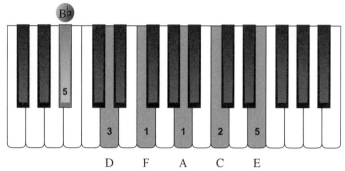

D F A C E

173

B♭maj¹³

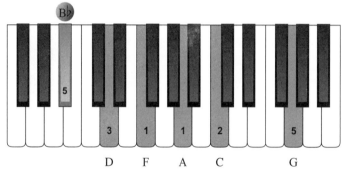

D F A C G

174

B♭maj¹³♭5

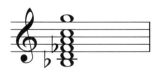

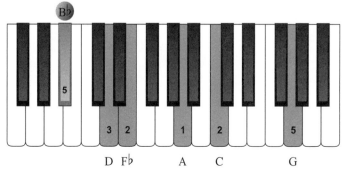

D F♭ A C G

175

B♭maj^{13#5}

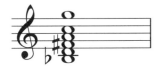

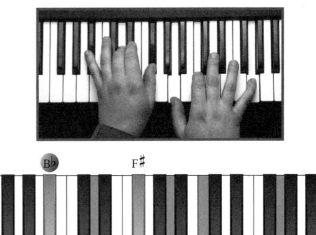

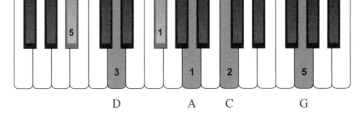

176

B♭maj^{13♭9}

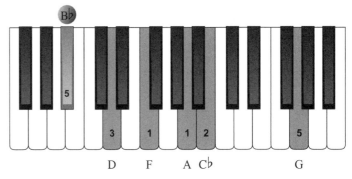

177

B♭maj^{13#9}

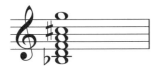

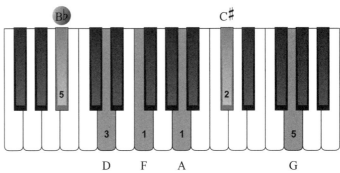

178

B♭m⁷♭⁹

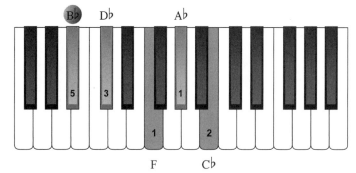

179

B♭m⁹

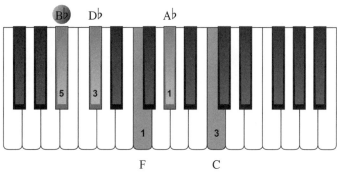

180

B♭m¹¹

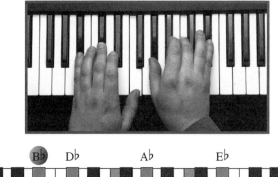

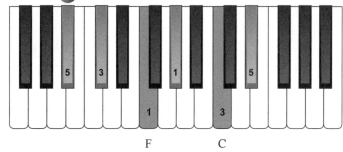

181

B

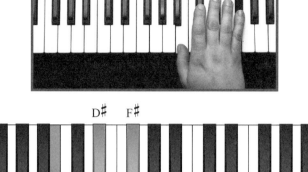

182

B+

183

B^{sus}4

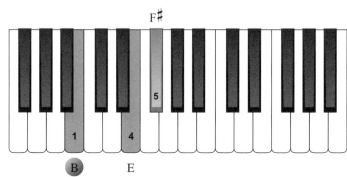

184

B⁶

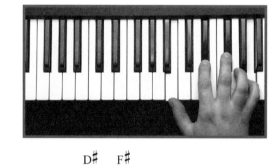

185

B⁷

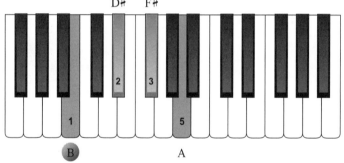

186

Bᴼ⁷

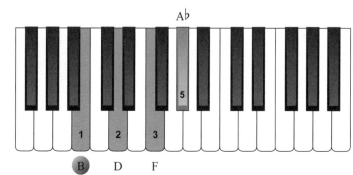

187

Bmaj⁷

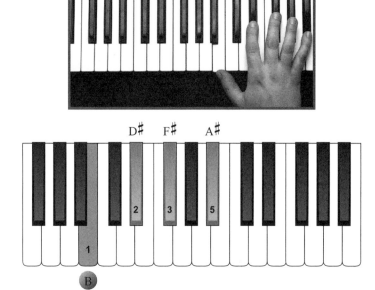

188

Bm

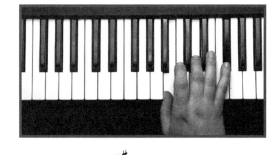

189

Bm⁶

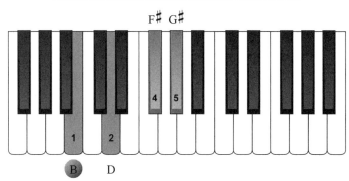

190

Bm⁷

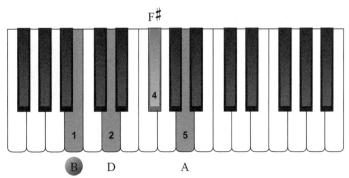

191

Bm⁷♭5

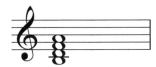

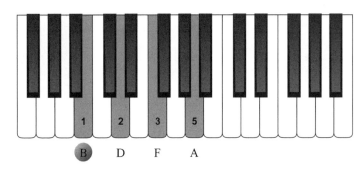

192

B⁷♭9

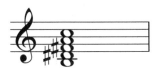

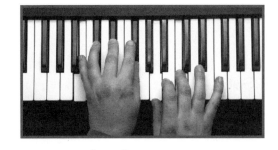

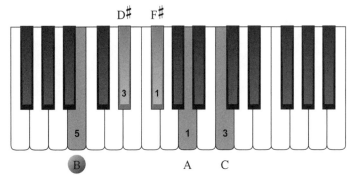

193

B⁷♯9

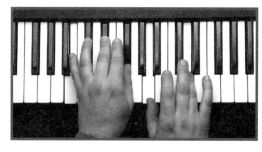

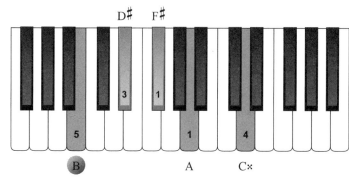

194

B⁹

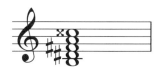

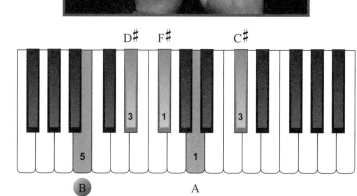

195

B⁹SUS4

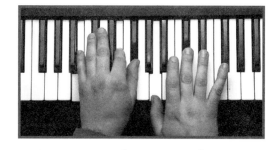

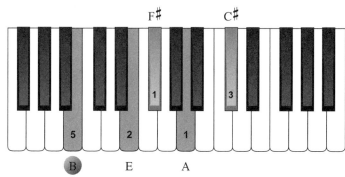

196

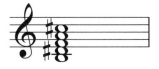

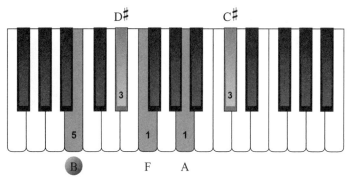

197

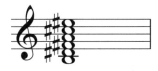

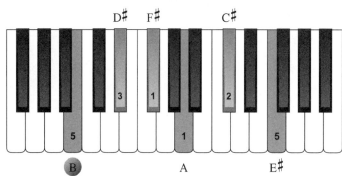

198

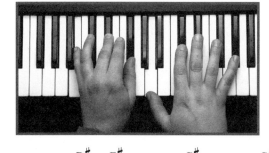

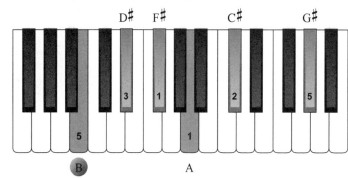

199

B^{13♭5}

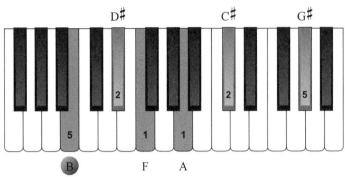

200

B^{13♭9}

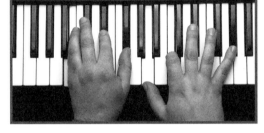

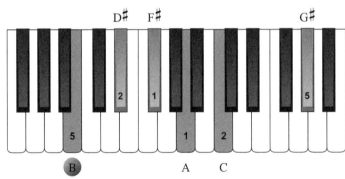

201

B^{13♯9}

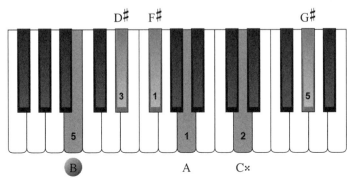

202

$B^{13\flat5\flat9}$

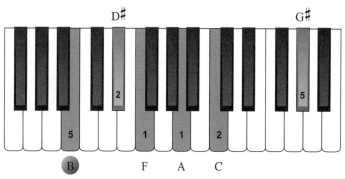

D#   G#

B   F   A   C

203

$B^{13\flat5\sharp9}$

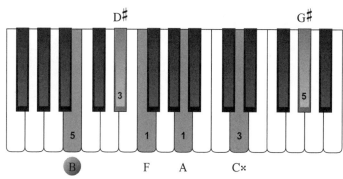

D#   G#

B   F   A   C×

204

$B^{13\sharp5\flat9}$

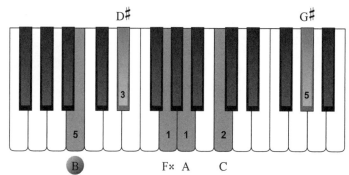

D#   G#

B   F× A   C

205

B¹³#5#9

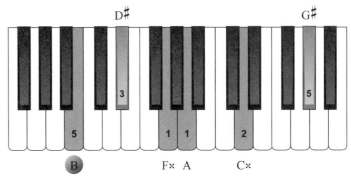

206

B⁶⁄₉

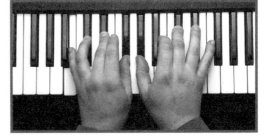

207

Bmaj⁹

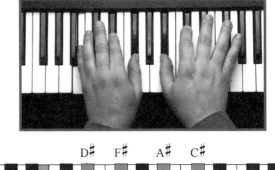

208

Bmaj⁹♯¹¹

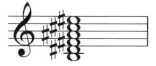

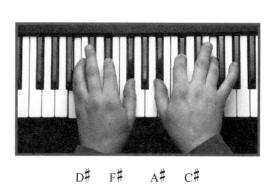

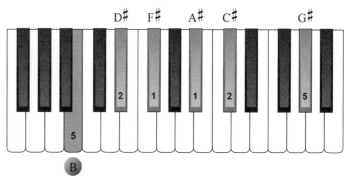

209

Bmaj¹³

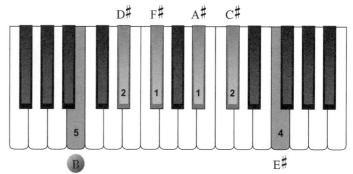

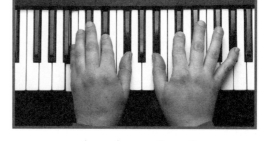

210

Bmaj¹³♭⁵

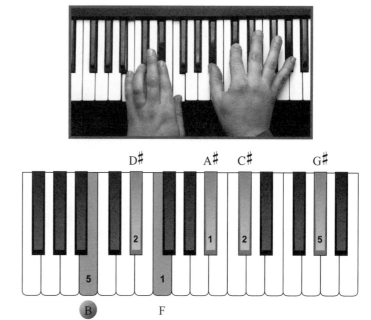

211

Bmaj^{13#5}

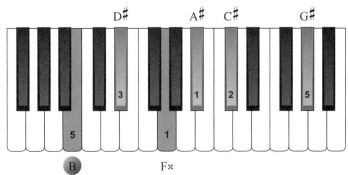

212

Bmaj^{13♭9}

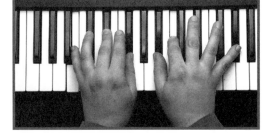

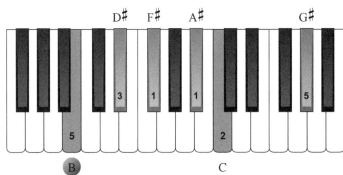

213

Bmaj^{13#9}

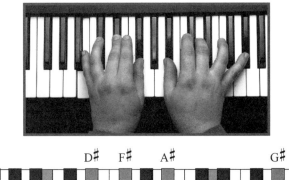

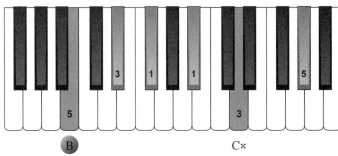

214

Bm⁷♭9

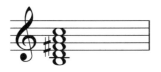

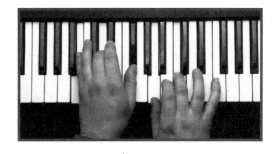

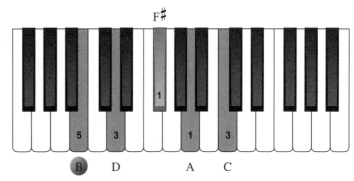

215

Bm⁹

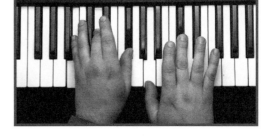

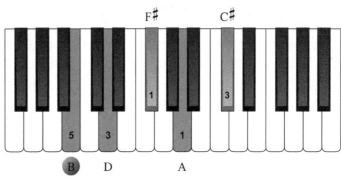

216

Bm¹¹

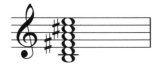

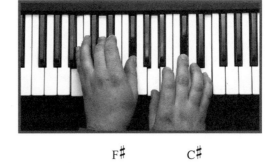

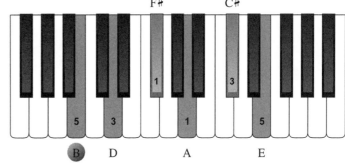

Your chord book comes with over 430 professional audio backing tracks. Hear each chord played note-by-note and together to help guide you to play them quickly and easily. Use your member number below to register on-line for lesson support at RockHouseMethod.com where you can download these tracks for FREE. Listen to them on your computer, download them to your portable device or burn them to a CD.

MEMBER NUMBER:
PK893256